Greetings from FLORIDA

Bob Morris

Soggy Cracker Press

Library of Congress catalog card number 82-61406

ISBN: 0-9607943-1-0

All work previously appeared in the Fort Myers News-Press. The author is grateful to Keith Moyer, Mike Vizvary, Maureen Downey, Laura Schwed and Larry Meyer for their editorial counsel and support. Thanks also to Laura Schwed for technical assistance and Barbara Havens for Exacto wizardry.

Cover design by Jim Mazzotta

First printing, September 1982
Great Outdoors Publishing Co.
St. Petersburg, Florida

A Soggy Cracker Press production

For all the Ohioans
who have stayed up there . . .

Introduction

Sometimes, living in Florida doesn't make even a little bit of sense.

You venture out at the height of the tourist season, and some bozo in a Winnebago flings you a finger-a-gram for so much as tooting at his kamikaze lane changing. Or it's March, and you stumble upon the whole grotesque spring-break beach scene, with its desperate sexuality amid the fetor of yesterday's lunch and beer shot from lips that probably recited poetry the week before at Ohio State, or maybe even Princeton. Or it's summer, and the heat is a liquid thing smelling of Big Macs and too many tires on too much asphalt, and all you can hear are rattling air conditioners, earth movers, cement trucks, transistor radios, dumb commercials. . . and some frail sanity warning that any compromise with Florida will, in the end, lay you to rest upon a shuffleboard court in some retirement village while angels hum "Where the Boys Are."

It can be crazy. The Florida existence demands (and requires) regular inspection. It can send folks like us searching.

That's why I like Bob Morris. More correctly, that's why I like the "writings" of Bob Morris. (I like Bob because he's a good family man, chews tobacco, says grace on Thanksgiving, swears with equal devoutness on other occasions, likes boats, dogs, mullet, hot greens, cold beer and baseball. Also, he has forgiven me for having once lived in Ohio as genuinely as I still forgive him for being a Florida Gator fan— God help the poor boy.)

Morris has the rare ability to distill this madness called "Life in Florida" into lucid — even rational — cubicles of experience. His typewriter mirrors our lives, and when we gaze into that mirror — lo and behold — there we are in our Bermuda shorts, pink flamingos poised, mullet nets in hand, ready to endure the worst that the condo builders, the mangrove killers, those Ohioans in Cadillacs and other Florida blighters have to offer. And, most startling of all, the mirror shows that we are laughing . . . at them and ourselves.

Nowhere is Bob's talent more evident than in this new book, "Greetings from Florida." In it, he writes about love, science, the failings of America's newspapers— and then turns his wit to more important matters. Inside, you will meet Cadwalder, who perceives a gigantic Commie plot at the very root of these prissy new diet fads. And you will visit again with the Largo Eight— that geriatric band of poker playing, diuretic guzzling jailbirds who had the gall to bellyache when the cops nailed them at their mobile home hideaway. You will learn how eating a plate of fried mullet can sometimes cure what penicillin can't, and you will come to understand why Drew Lee Bonkers is the closest thing Yalahahumpka, Florida has to a real live celebrity— next to Simp Simpson's cauliflower, that is.

So, if the Florida Madness occasionally shadows you, sends you scanning for method and reason in a land of Steubinville-By-The-Sea, disco drunk factories and other tacky postcard attractions, then I highly recommend this book. It's easier than visiting a psychiatrist, and cheaper than a moving van headed for Paducah.

"Greetings From Florida" is Bob Morris at his best. And that is very good, indeed. . .

Randy White
Hendry Creek
August, 1982

Foreword

To understand the thoughts behind this book, it would help for you to see the place where I work.

I hesitate to call it an office. Rather, it is a corner, an altogether nice corner to one side of the newsroom, with a consistently cluttered desk, a cantankerous IBM Selectric typewriter, a hopelessly filthy spittoon and three or four cardboard boxes filled up with important stuff that defies all attempts to be properly filed away.

But most striking of all — I'm reluctant to call them attractive without some qualification — are the tacky postcards. There are dozens of them, in all degrees of gaudiness, taped to the glass partitions that form my corner.

I've forgotten exactly how I came to collect them. I think friends must have sent me the first ones when I was new at the paper and I put them up just to give my little corner that sense of identity which is so important to someone who is fresh out of college and starting his first real job.

That was seven years ago and I guess I just got carried away. I stuck around this place and now the tacky postcards are everywhere. I have to peek between their edges to get a glimpse of what's going on outside of my corner.

Specifically, they are tacky Florida postcards. And even more specifically than that, they are tacky Florida postcards that feature alligators of every description and women in skimpy bathing suits. In many of the postcards, the alligators are actually attempting to bite the women in skimpy bathing suits. I like to specialize.

And I like to think that to understand Florida you have to understand the beauty of a tacky postcard. Believe me, it's something that grows on you.

This is a state that demands of its residents an acceptance of its dual nature.

It is in the South, yet not wholly of the South. Tract homes for transplanted Midwesterners sprout up next to Cracker homesteads. You can find grits, bagels and cafe con leche all on the same block; hear "y'all," "youse guys" and "mis amigos" in a single conversation.

Pot smugglers make clandestine air drops in scrub forests where moonshine stills are not unheard of. Surfers slice the waves while wheelchair-bound retirees look on.

For every supreme sunset there's a condo rising to block the view. And each time a jet screams above the Everglades a lone panther cocks its head to listen.

It is contrast that makes a tacky postcard tacky. And it is contrast that makes Florida, well, Florida. You cannot have it any other way.

The stories in this book are not unlike brief messages on the back of tacky postcards. Most were dashed off on the spur of the moment. And none of them will take you more than a few minutes to read.

I have my favorites, of course. The stories on themes that are intrinsically Floridian — mullet, tourists, plastic flamingos — are just plain fun to write about, especially if I can milk them for a laugh. Other stories, about love or politics or social customs, might not seem unique to Florida. But I assure you they are, by virtue of perspective. We do see things a bit differently down here, you know. It comes from having to peek out from behind the postcards.

At any rate, greetings from Florida.

Having a great time. Glad you are here.

Bob Morris
August 1982

Greetings From Florida

Do you know how many Ohioans it takes to change a light bulb? Five. One to change it and four to stand around complaining about how they never burn out back up home.

To: Gil and Gert Gruntstone
111 Buckeye Place
Mostanywhere, Ohio

Dear Gil and Gert,
Greetings from Florida!

Hope you like this jumbo, 3-D postcard which cost us $2.75 at the same store where Mildred bought some real nice sunglasses with sea shells all over them and I got a genuine beaded Indian belt.

It says "Made in Taiwan" on the inside of the belt, but the man at the cash register told me that "Taiwan" is the name of some big Indian reservation out in the middle of the Everglades. I sure hope we can visit it.

Gil, I thought you would get a big kick out of this postcard. To fully appreciate it what you have to do is hold it up in the light and move it back and forth so it makes it look like the alligator is chomping down on that girl in the bikini. Isn't that a sight!

I know you can't find anything like this card back up home, even if you go into Sandusky. I bet the guys down at the VFW will get a big laugh out of it, too.

They had some other good postcards at this store. One of them shows another alligator chomping down on some girl in a bikini with the words: "We Florida alligators would rather bite than switch" coming out of the alligator's mouth. Isn't that a laugh and a half?

I also bought this one that showed a real pretty girl wearing the skimpiest blouse I've ever seen and she was holding two giant grapefruit out in front of her. But Midlred said it was too suggestive and probably wouldn't even get through the mail.

When she wasn't looking I went ahead and bought it anyway

though. I'll bring them all back home and we can have a showing of them down at the VFW some night. Won't that be a time? Whooooooeee!

We've had nothing but a good vacation except for the day we spent in Miami. You know, it is hard to find anyone who speaks English down there. Mildred and I went into this store to buy some corn plasters and when I asked the lady clerk for help all she could give me was some of this foreign talk I didn't understand.

Well, you know I fought in Double-U, Double-U Two and spent a little time in France where I picked up the language, so I said to this lady: "Como-tally-view?" That just seemed to get her more riled up and I'm still not sure what she said as we were going out the door, but I think it was vicious enough to make the paint peel off the walls and we never did get the corn plasters.

Came across some real nice folks though in a place called LaBelle where we stopped at this little restaurant for breakfast. I should mention that Mildred has been troubled by all the bugs down here biting her and she has been swollen up something awful with bumps all over her and everything.

We walked into this restaurant and our waitress asked Mildred: "Honey, what is wrong with you?"

And Mildred started right in complaining about all the bugs. Then she started complaining about the heat and the humidity and the traffic and how we don't have any of these problems back up home. She was still complaining when the waitress brought our food.

I looked down on our plates and I noticed this pile of white stuff like oatmeal that I had never seen before and I asked the waitress: "What is this?"

But before the waitress could answer, this fellow sitting at the counter spoke up and said: "Y'all folks are in luck. That white stuff is called 'grits' and it just happens to be the best mosquito repellant known unto man. Here, let me show you how it works."

And with that this fellow came over to our table and started smearing this "grits" stuff all over Mildred and I.

Well, at first I thought this was peculiar, but everyone in the restaurant assured us that we don't dare step out in Florida anymore unless we have grits smeared all over us. They were so nice they even let us buy a bag of these grits for $25. Normally grits are in such short supply, the people told us, they sell for upwards of $50 for a one-pound bag.

Anyway, Mildred and I boil up a little every morning and put it all over our arms and legs and faces and it has worked just fine. Every now and then we get some strange looks, but I would rather have strange looks than mosquito bites any day.

Well, looks like I am running out of room on this jumbo, 3-D postcard which I bought for $2.75.

See you when we get home. Wish you were here. Ha-Ha.
Love,
Fred and Mildred

Real Florida Hospitality

This is for everyone who believes that house-guests are like fish. Unless you get rid of them, they stink after a couple of days.

A reader has come to me for advice. This fact alone should tell you how desperate the poor fellow is.

"I need help in a very ticklish situation," the reader tells me. "I have lived down here for several years now and I don't think a month has gone by that I haven't had visitors of some sort dropping in for their vacations.

"At first, I didn't mind so much. But it gets old after awhile, especially when the visitors stay and stay and stay, demanding to be entertained and eating me out of house and home.

"I think you could provide a great service by devoting a column to 'How Floridians Should Deal With Undesirable House Guests.' Please do it soon as I am going broke and crazy."

Since this is a matter of utmost concern to untold millions of Floridians, I'll oblige with pleasure, sir.

The first thing you must do is determine exactly who is an "Undesirable House Guest" and who is a "Desirable House Guest."

Here are some guidelines:

Desirable House Guest: Greets you by saying, "What's the best restaurant in town? I'm taking you there tonight."

Undesirable House Guest: Greets you by saying, "How long will it take you to drive us to Disney World tomorrow morning?"

Desirable House Guest: After getting unpacked says, "Here's a couple of hundred bucks to cover our expenses."

Undesirable House Guest: After getting unpacked says,

"Would you mind turning the thermostat down to 65? I hate the heat and humidity. And by the way, I like to eat dinner by 6 p.m."

Desirable House Guest: Leaves by saying: "Here's a key to our cabin up in the mountains. Feel free to use it anytime."

Undesirable House Guest: Leaves by saying: "See you next year."

A successful assault against the Undesirable House Guest requires great cunning. Reverse psychology works well. I have found the "Smother Them With Hospitality" ploy to be quite effective.

When your guests arrive, greet them warmly and cheerfully announce that you have taken time off from work just to show them around. Don't allow them time to unpack. That only encourages them to stay longer. Immediately pile them into your car and begin showing them the sights.

A sample itinerary:

Day 1:A picnic in the Everglades. This is best between April and October when your guests are likely to fall victim to heat prostration and require prolonged hospital care at their own expense. Make sure you don't pack mosquito repellant or water or a snake bite kit. If your guests have children, suggest they wade the canals and investigate the "mysterious floating logs."

Venture down side roads, especially roads that look particularly muddy. If you are lucky, you will get stuck. Some local resident with a swamp buggy will come along and pull you out. For this service he will charge $100. Of course, you will have forgotten your wallet.

Day 2: Give them breakfast in bed. At 4 a.m. Then it's off for a day at the beach.

Tell your guests: "Thanks to the peculiar geographical and climatic conditions in Florida it is impossible to get sunburned, so just frolic to your heart's content without any of that sticky, smelly sun screen." Then wait for the fun to start.

Try to pick an area that is highly developed with lots of those interval ownership condo salesmen hustling the beach trying to suck people into buying one of those joints. If you are lucky, your guests will buy one and never bother you again.

Leave your car parked in the bright sun with all the windows rolled up. Make sure your guests sit down on the vinyl seat covers without protection from any beach towels. Then listen to them sizzle.

That night, while they are in the shower, dump a little sand in the bed.

Day 3: Greet them with a hearty slap on the back and then head off for a trip in your boat.

If your boat is like every other boat, something always goes wrong. Maybe you will capsize. If you aren't that fortunate, then at least the motor will blow up and you will drift aimlessly until midnight and everyone will whine and complain until someone comes along and tows you in. They, too, will charge $100. Ooops, forgot that wallet again.

Even the most Undesirable House Guest is quick to leave before Day 4 comes along. But if, by some chance, they should still be there when you wake up, then just tell them they're in luck because you've arranged a walking tour of downtown Miami at midnight.

That should clear them out in a hurry and you'll be free and clear until the next horde rolls in.

Wisdom From Ol' Barefoot

I don't mind saying that this is a plug for Tom Gaskins and his Cypress Knee Museum. If you want to learn about Florida, then just drive to Palmdale and let Tom educate you. There ain't nothing Mickey Mouse about his place.

I jumped out of a canoe last week and landed on an oyster bar. I wasn't wearing any shoes. My feet wound up looking like I'd used an electric fan for a pedicure.

As everyone knows, oyster bars contain oyster shells and oyster shells are covered with all sorts of goop and grunge. When this goop and grunge gets into cuts it proceeds to do some wicked work.

What it did to my feet was make them swell up so bad it looked as if I was walking on a couple of those fat sausages you see hanging from the ceiling at an Italian butcher shop. I couldn't even look at a pair of shoes, much less wear them.

At first, this appeared to be a major setback. While I am a firm believer in casual attire for all occasions, I generally follow convention when it comes to shoes. I didn't look forward to going shoeless.

But one morning, while my feet were still hurting something fierce, I had to go to the store. Driving home, I had a flat tire. I checked the spare. It was flat, too. I had to walk the half mile or so home. Barefoot.

It turned out to be a wonderful stroll. I walked on the pavement and when it got hot I walked in mud puddles. Then I walked on grass to scrape off the mud and enjoy a gentle massage.

There is something liberating about going barefoot. It makes you feel like a kid again.

Better than that, going barefoot is therapeutic. It restores good health. By the time I got home my feet were feeling just fine.

A miracle cure? I think so. But before I decided to go public with this remarkable discovery, I consulted an expert, Ol' Barefoot himself, Tom Gaskins.

You've read about Tom Gaskins in this column before. He and his family live over in Palmdale at the big bend in U.S. 27 where they run the world famous Cypress Knee Museum. Tom Gaskins knows more about cypress trees and swamps than any man alive. He is an authority on hunting wild turkeys and conservative politics and alligators and more stuff than there's room to mention here.

Tom Gaskins is also the premier great thinker of the barefoot philosophy. He grew up going barefoot in Florida and, at 73 years old, he still doesn't wear shoes, not even on the daily 3-5 mile run that helps him stay skinny and fit.

"Oh, I'll wear them if there's a funeral or a wedding or I have to go to court. But other than that I don't ever put 'em on," he told me. "The only pair I've got I bought 10 years ago and they are just like new. Black laceups. I hate 'em."

Since I'm a novice in this barefoot business, I asked Tom to give me all the reasons why people should forsake their shoes. Let me share some of them:

Economy— "Shoes cost money. Bare feet don't."

Hunting and Fishing— "If you have to wade in the water and you're wearing shoes, then your feet will stay wet all day. This isn't healthy. Bare feet dry right off."

Longevity— "Figure that a pair of shoes weighs about one pound. Figure that if you're an active person you pick up your feet 5,000 times a day. This is two-and-a-half tons of picking up. You're saving strength if you go barefoot."

Agility— "You go barefoot long enough and your feet grow wider and longer. This gives you better balance. They also grow more agile. If I drop a dime I can pick it up with my toes. This saves me from bending over."

Air Pollution— "If you wear shoes, then your feet stink. You go barefoot and they get a chance to air out. Most people can appreciate this."

The only thing that worries Tom about going barefoot is that it sometimes presents a danger if he's working with electricity.

"I'm real careful with electricity," he said. "It scares me. My feet ain't that tough."

I asked him what he thought about walking barefoot on oyster bars.

"Only a damn fool would do that," he said.

He's right.

How To Become A Southerner

I forgot to mention it in this column, but it also helps if, given the choice, you never choose hash brown potatoes instead of grits.

A reader with a problem has asked me for some help. His name is Danny Marsh.

Since Danny's problem is one that is no doubt shared by many of you who have come to live in this part of the country, I have devoted today's column to solving it once and for all.

I'll let Danny explain the problem.

"I want to renounce my previous Yankee statehood," Danny writes. "Somehow I was born in the wrong part of the country. I had no choice in the matter. However, after I became wise and realized my true nature I took action. I got in the car and beelined it south.

"I love it in Florida. I divorced my Yankee wife and married a soft Florida woman. I act like a gentleman at all times. I don't talk loud or fast. When I visit relatives in the deranged North I realize two things— I'm glad I live in Florida and those Yankees can be an oafish lot.

"If I had a choice I would have been born here. Should I be eternally punished for the errors of my parents?

"A person can become a naturalized citizen of the United States. They take a test and an oath. A judge then proclaims them a United States citizen. They become one of us.

"I want to become a naturalized southerner. I'm ready to renounce all Yankee ties, attitudes and allegiances. I promise never to utter: 'Back up north...' "

"But what is the rest? Who can administer the oath to become a naturalized Southerner? What are the requirements? Your thoughts on this problem would be greatly appreciated."

Well, Danny, my thoughts on the problem run something like this: The last thing I want to do is promote sectionalism. I mean, the War Between the States has been over for more than a century and we're just one big, happy country now. Right?

But since you seem so distraught and knowing full well that there are others who share your predicament, then far be it from me to let you continue to suffer.

As it turns out, there are certain hard-and-fast requirements for becoming a naturalized Southerner. And it looks as if you have already met a number of them.

Of course, when it comes to marital status, that's a matter of personal preference and doesn't really effect your Southern citizenship. However, I laud your choice in picking a soft woman. The hard ones can bruise you.

The fact that you "act like a gentleman at all times" is also commendable. But I should point out that acting like a gentleman and actually being a gentleman are two entirely different matters and maybe you should work on that.

You mention that you "don't talk loud and fast." Now, I understand what you're saying here. You mean you don't talk loud and fast in normal conversation or in any way that could be construed as rude, offensive and harsh to the ear. That's fine. But you should make note that, as a Southerner, there are numerous situations that call for loud and fast talking. Lying and arguing, all noble Southern traits, fall into this category.

As for never beginning your sentences by saying — "Back up north" — again, I applaud your reform. But there are a couple of exceptions where this phrase is acceptable. For instance, it's OK if you say "Back up north... in Atlanta" or "Back up north... where I got caught for trucking in illegal cigarettes and liquor."

Now that those minor details are out of the way, you are welcome to take this short, multiple-choice quiz, just so we can make sure you meet all the requirements of Southern citizenship.

1.Name three inalienable rights:

a.Life, liberty and the pursuit of happiness.

b.Fishing, drinking and a pickup with four wheel drive.

2.The three main branches of government are:

a.Executive, judicial and legislative.

b.Doesn't matter long as you've got a friend down at the courthouse.

3.Who is the current chief executive?

a.Ronald Reagan

b.Bear Bryant

4.Choose the answer which best describes the National Anthem:

a."The Star Spangled Banner," written by Francis Scott Key while he watched the battle at Fort McHenry in Baltimore.

b.The title doesn't matter so much as long as the song was recorded in Nashville, tells about loving-cheating-drinking-fighting-trucks-trains and appears on the juke box at my favorite bar.

5.The document that is the framework for our way of life is:

a.The Constitution

b.The Sears-Roebuck Catalogue

Now raise your right hand and repeat after me: "I solemnly swear."

That's it for the oath, but at this point you may solemnly swear and cuss the Yankee citizenship out of your system in whatever way you like.

You are now a Southern citizen.

Don't let us down.

Thou Shalt Not Tax My Beer

I'm proud to pay my taxes. But I could be just as proud for half the money.

News item: "President Reagan is considering an increase in so-called 'sin taxes,' administration officials said Tuesday. If approved, the federal tax on cigarettes, liquor, beer and wine could double."

Dear President Reagan,

Let me begin by saying thanks for the recent income tax cut.

It's been in effect for almost a month now and, as a result, my disposable income has increased by a whopping $4.50 a week.

I was all set to celebrate this windfall, maybe throw a party or something, when I read about your latest idea. Let's just say I was less than enthusiastic about the proposal to double the federal tax on booze and cigarettes.

I did a little calculating with some information from the Bureau of Alcohol, Tobacco and Firearms. I figure that if this proposal went into effect and I threw a modest party to celebrate my modest income tax break — using say, four quarts of liquor, two cases of beer and two gallons of wine— it would cost me an extra $12.22 in taxes.

Here's a breakdown: Each quart of liquor would cost $2.65 more. Each case of beer would cost 64 cents more. And each gallon of wine would cost 17 cents more.

I don't smoke cigarettes, but some of my friends do. Under this proposal, my friends would be paying eight cents more for each pack.

I think you'd have to agree that there's no sense in celebrating with figures like this.

Frankly, Mr. President, the idea of doubling taxes on booze and cigarettes is the dumbest proposal I've heard in a long time. With the economy going the way it is, there's damn little your average working person can rejoice in. After putting in a full day on the job at salaries that aren't keeping up with inflation, we deserve to take a little nip and enjoy a smoke. It helps make high interest rates and grocery prices seem a little less awful.

Now I'm all with you in your effort to balance the federal budget. But I don't think this is the way to do it. I'd like to point out that about a month ago the Russians got into a similar budget dilemma and immediately responded by doubling the price of vodka and cigarettes. I don't think you'd want to be accused of following their example.

Don't get me wrong. I'm all for increasing the "sin tax." It's just that I don't consider the use of alcohol and cigarettes to be sinful.

I know a lot of people would probably disagree with me on that point, but I can only refer to a highly-acclaimed set of rules on the subject of sin. You can look it up in your Bible. It's in Exodus, Chapter 20, verses 1 through 17. It's popularly called the Ten Commandments.

Now, if we're going to get serious about this so-called "sin tax" let's use the Ten Commandments as our guide.

First of all, please notice that there's no mention anywhere in the Ten Commandments about booze and cigarettes.

But not to worry. There are plenty of real sins that are ripe for taxing. Indeed, if you decided to pursue this "sin tax" to the fullest degree, then the federal coffers could soon be overflowing. And we wouldn't even have to tax all 10 of the sins set down in the Commandments. Just a few of the juicy ones would get the job done.

Take "Thou shalt not commit adultery," for example. Now, heh-heh, I don't need to tell you that there's a whole lot of this adultery business going on these days and the federal government isn't getting a cent from it. A straightforward tax of, say, $10 per extramarital affair seems fair and reasonable.

Then there's "Thou shalt not bear false witness against thy neighbor." What this boils down to, plain and simple, is gossip and idle rumor. Great potential here. Every time the National Enquirer hits the newsstand, there'd be more bucks rolling into the federal treasury. Rona Barret would be a big contributor, too.

As for, "Thou shalt not steal" and "Thou shalt not kill," well, these are naturals. Thieves and murderers seldom carry their fair burden of the tax load and this could quickly recitfy that sorry situation.

The country seems to be filled with smart-aleck kids. Put a punitive tax bite behind "Honor thy father and mother" and we've got that problem taken care of quite nicely.

Let's not forget "Thou shalt not take the Lord's name in vain." If a tax on this sin had been in effect the day it was announced you were considering doubling the tax on booze and cigarettes, then we would have had enough revenues to retire the national debt.

At this point, you are probably thinking: "Great idea, but how are we going to enforce these commandments and collect on all the sinning that's going on?"

Simple.

There's an organization that in recent months has done a whole lot of talking about sin in this country. I guarantee that if you got in touch with your buddies in the Moral Majority they'd jump at the chance to regulate the new "sin tax." Shoot, they'd probably do it for free.

So please give my suggestions serious consideration. If you come through I'll invite you to my celebration party.

Your pal,
Bob Morris

A Little Help From Drew Lee

Not long after this column appeared, Lovie Sue quit Drew Lee and went to work on the professional mud wrastlin' circuit. She teams up with Silas the hog. Mo Stunkwilder hasn't told a joke since. And I never did get my free windshield cleaning.

'Lo there, y'all. Drew Lee Bonkers is the name and writing a newspaper column ain't really my game.

This is just a favor I am doing for my longtime buddy and faithful admirer, ol' Bob what's-his-face. Bob called me up and said he'd come down with a "writer's block" and would I mind writing something in his place to keep his bosses happy.

I don't know what a "writer's block" is or even if it's contagious. All I know is that Bob went out to eat at a Mexican restaurant over the weekend with his wife and some friends and they got in a contest to see who could eat the most jalapeno peppers and Bob won.

The "writer's block" appeared shortly after the pepper-eating contest, which I think is kind of strange since it has always been my experience that the last thing jalapeno peppers will do you is stop you up.

Knowing Bob, he probably complicated his digestive matters by sipping on some of that cactus juice that Mexicans like to drink. Trouble with cactus juice is that after drinking a little of it you want to run around yapping and howling like a dog.

This can be dangerous in a Mexican restaurant. You run around yapping and howling like a dog and you'll wind up chopped and fried with a tortilla wrapped around you.

Now, I'm not saying this is the way it is in every Mexican restaurant. All I'm saying is that you drive across the border to Juarez or someplace and put your pet poodle out on the street and see how long it lasts. That's all I'm saying.

Maybe I should tell you something about me since I'm the fellow who's in charge of this newspaper column today. You have probably read about me in here before because every time

Bob needs an authority on beer or women or fishing or beer or politics or football or beer I'm the one he calls on.

I'll admit it. I am something of a genius.

I am also a gin-u-ine business ty-coon. Got me a store up in Yalahahumpka with a big ol' sign outside that says: "Drew Lee's Tru-Lee Fine Emporium." And then, in little squiggly letters under that it says: "General Merchandise, Bait & Tackle, Bar & Grill, Gas & Oil, This & That."

I am also the general postmaster, the Noter Republic, the local Amway distributor and a special deputized sheriff with a card in my wallet and everything.

Round Yalahahumpka I'm the closest thing there is to a celebrity, not counting Simp Simpson who got written up in some farm magazine after he grew a giant cauliflower that bore an uncanny resemblance to Elvis Presley. That was a couple of years ago and Simp's fame has all but died out although I understand he has trained his champeen hog, Silas, to wear a leotard and roll around in the mud whenever Simp turns his teevee on to the "Richard Simmons Show." I haven't seen Silas perform as of yet, but I hear it is some kind of sight and will probably make Simp even more famous than before.

But back to me and this newspaper column. Bob said if I couldn't think of anything serious to write about I could always just tell a joke which is what I think I'll do. I hear a lot of them from Mo Stunkwilder who spends his days sitting out front of my store watching Lovie Sue Stegall pump gas.

I hired Lovie Sue a year or so ago when this big discount gas station opened up down the road and started selling gas at a dime a gallon cheaper than me. Lovie Sue is 19-years-old and can do things to a t-shirt that should be against the law. She is the kind of girl who could make you leave your wife and kids and start robbing liquor stores for a living.

All I know is that Lovie Sue put that big discount gas station out of business all by herself and I am now charging $5 if you want your windshield wiped.

Mo Stunkwilder sits out front drinking Nehis and tries to sweeten Lovie Sue up by telling her jokes. This is one I heard the other day which I will tell because it is about the only clean one I've ever heard out of Mo.

Mo says: "Lovie Sue, you know why cream costs so much more than milk?"

Lovie Sue says: "No, Mo. Why's that?"

Mo says: "Because them cows just hate squatting down over those tiny little containers."

Jokes like that are one reason why Mo Stunkwilder won't get any further than just sitting on a bench and watching Lovie Sue.

I have just gone back and counted up all my words and am proud to report that I have reached the point where I can quit.

There ain't much to this newspaper column business and I can't believe ol' Bob actually gets paid for this.

I hope he gets over his "writer's block." Think I'll give him a gift certificate entitling him to a free windshield wiping courtesy of Lovie Sue. Guarantee you he can write something about that.

The Joy Of Farming

I'm not much of a farmer. My last backyard garden was so bad that the neighborhood rabbit had to go on welfare.

Seeking to add gentility and self-sufficiency to my life, I set out some months ago to become a Gentleman Farmer.

My quest was both poetic and pragmatic.

On the one hand, I sought to renew my bond with the soil, to engage in the timeless tradition of tilling the land, of reaping what I sowed.

That was the poetic part.

On the other hand, I was damn tired of paying $1.49 for a mottled head of cauliflower and settling for tomatoes that tasted as if they'd been shot up with sawdust.

That was the pragmatic part.

I think anyone who sets out to become a Gentleman Farmer would do well to keep in mind these two divergent parts of the total horticultural picture. It helps maintain a balance, not to mention a pleasant temperment, a healthy blood pressure and sanity.

One cannot risk being too pragmatic when it comes to growing vegetables, because when bugs and disease arrive, as surely they will, it pays to accept them poetically — as gentle agents of nature, as fellow travelers through the universe — and not worry unduly about the dollars and cents of their destruction.

By the same token, one dare not go overboard in the poetic direction, but should, instead, invest pragmatically in poisons and insecticides to annihilate these nasty vermin, or else prepare one's self to go hungry.

This much said on the philosophy of gardening, I will now offer brief instruction on how you may come to know, as I have, the joys of the Gentleman Farmer.

FINDING THE RIGHT PLACE FOR YOUR BACK YARD GARDEN—I think it's abundantly obvious that the right place for your back yard garden is, indeed, the back yard. There are many reasons for this, one being that if you should plant your garden in the front yard and it turns out, by some miracle, to be a bountiful plot, then you stand to lose a good portion of your harvest to vagrant pilferers— the mailman, the Avon lady, Jehovah's Witnesses and so on. But the best reason for planting your garden in the back yard is a simple matter of social preservation. In all likelihood, your garden will not turn out to be the showpiece you'd like it to be — the pole beans barren, the zucchini sterile— and by choosing a low profile back yard location there is less chance for your peers to see it and, in turn, make mockery of your ineffectual efforts.

Some of you might not have a back yard. I am thinking specificially of certain Third World people, confined to meager hovels in the downscale neighborhoods of their teeming cities. If this be the case, you may simply farm the floor of your hut, letting the sun shine in through the roof as it no doubt already does and through this ingenious method rid yourself of both the problems mentioned above. One further consolation— very few rabbits surv ive in neighborhoods such as yours.

PREPARING THE SOIL — Those of you who've tried to use a simple hoe to turn a yard that has been planted with Bahia grass, know the inherent futility of such a venture. What you need is a wondrous device known as a Rototiller. Once you crank up a Rototiller and go to work it is like unleashing 10 million moles on amphetamines. A word of caution. One Gentleman Farmer of my acquaintance, who shall remain anonymous, set out with a Rototiller to create a small 10 X 20 plot and, unable to keep the beast in rein, wound up plowing gardens for five of his adjacent neighbors. The case is still being settled in court.

FERTILIZER—You will need lots of this because, sad to say, Mother Earth is not the gal she used to be. In fact, in certain locales she has witnessed the change of life and without a little motivation is altogether unresponsive. There are two types of fertilizer. One is mostly chemicals and the other is organic. The significant difference between them is that organic fertilizer stinks the most. Feel free to make your own choice, but remember, after a good, hard rain the aroma of animal waste is not the most pleasing fragrance one could hope for and could lead to petitions for your banishment from the neighborhood.

WHEN TO QUIT—With a little luck, even the worst of gardens should provide you with food for the table. But, as in everything, there are limits to how far you should go with this Gentleman Farmer business. As a rule of thumb, it is time to quit when, out of homage to the old adage "Waste not, want not," you have not only made eggplant cookies, but are thinking about experimenting with collard green pie.

The Kindest Cut Of All

Sydney's voice is about three octaves higher these days. Still, he seems happy, now that he doesn't worry about women.

The trouble with Sydney is that he's lonesome. Whenever he's lonesome he paces the floor and howls.

There's not much else he can do actually, so I try my best not to criticize him for it. It wouldn't do any good. Cats don't listen to criticism.

They don't listen to threats either. I have tried to threaten Sydney.

"Listen, pal," I told him, "if you don't stop howling I'm going to make you go out, get a job and start supporting yourself around here."

He responded with a howl in my face. Not only is Sydney shiftless, but he's cocky.

I guess if I was a tomcat and I was lonesome, then I would howl, too. I mean, it's not like Sydney can just call up an old girlfriend or go cruise a singles bar, although I can envision him strolling up to a fluffy little number and purring something smooth like "I love the way you twitch your tail, honey."

But these aren't among his options. When he gets lonesome all he can do is pace the floor and howl. Lately he's been howling all the time. He must be very lonesome.

Actually, I am trying to be delicate about this and lonesome is the delicate description of his problem.

More precisely, Sydney is lonesome for a female cat. Even more precisely, he is ripe with lust.

I cannot be much more precise than that within the confines of your basic family newspaper, but I think you get the picture. Sydney is howling for good reason.

As I write this, Sydney is downstairs pacing the living room floor and doing his routine at full pitch. Mere words cannot adequately describe this sound, but I will give it a try.

Imagine yourself on a camping trip in the deep woods. Just as you slip off to sleep, there erupts from the darkness a terribly haunting and blood-curdling howl. Your tentmate says: "Go shine the flashlight and see what that is." You say: "Forget it. I'm not going anywhere near whatever that noise came from."

That's kind of what it sounds like when Sydney howls. It starts from deep within and rolls out in a long, scary moan of startling volume.

It is enough to make the neighbors complain, which they do with understandable consternation. It is enough to rouse you from a deep sleep, which it does with infuriating regularity. And it is enough to make it totally impossible to maintain peace of mind in your own home, which it is doing at this very moment.

I am not going to say that Sydney has driven me completely crazy with this howling, but given time he will surely get me there. Therefore, I am attempting to protect what little sanity I have left.

Now, there are two things you can do when a tomcat has the problem that Sydney seems to be having. One is a perfectly natural thing that involves an obliging female cat with the result being a litter of little Sydneys. The other is a rather unnatural thing that involves a veterinarian's scalpel with the result being that there will never ever be another litter of little Sydneys.

I have tried the first thing, because I consider the second thing rather drastic, not to mention painful. I found Sydney this cute little Siamese and the two of them did some serious courting for a couple of days. If everything works out, the kittens should arrive in April.

I thought Sydney would be thankful for this kindness I showed him and would demonstrate his gratitude by clamming up. But he is howling worse than ever before. I guess that once you go to the well, you get hooked on the water.

I truly do not like the idea of the second thing, Sydney, but I'm afraid you've left me little choice. Maybe it won't be so bad. You'll grow fat and happy and won't worry about women anymore. There's a lot to be said for that, I suppose, although I wouldn't want it for myself.

The pamphlet from the veterinarian makes it sound OK: "Recovery from anesthesia is quite rapid, the hospital stay is relatively short and healing is usually prompt."

So howl on while you can, buddy. Very soon I will offer you up to what — for my ears at least — will be the kindest cut of all.

Life With Boswell

Boswell has a pedigree. All this means is that we had to pay big money before he could chew up the sofa.

I was watching the late movie when I came to the conclusion that life with Boswell will be forever, uh, interesting.

The movie was "Beach Party," with Frankie Avalon and Annette Funicello. Annette had just slapped Frankie for being fresh when suddenly the picture went fuzzy.

I got up and turned some knobs, but the problem wasn't with the adjustments.

The problem was with the cable. More to the point, the problem was with the cable that was dangling from Boswell's mouth.

I stood there watching as he bit down a final time— chomp— and the cable snapped in two. No more "Beach Party."

I don't think for a moment that Boswell was being malicious.

No, I prefer to believe that he was merely making a social statement regarding late-night television and B-grade movies.

I will admit, however, that he has a strange way of expressing himself. Some of his social statements far exceed my understanding. Maybe that's just his metaphysical nature. If Boswell were an artist— which I'm not so sure he isn't— he would be an abstract expressionist.

That's why I don't know what it means when he:

- Attacks the vacuum cleaner when my wife is trying to tidy the living room carpet. He also attacks the broom when she is trying to sweep the kitchen floor.
- Raids my garden and destroys the tomatoes. The plants on the porch are showing the wounds of his fury, too.
- Nibbles on my favorite shoes. I've heard of fetishes, but this is kinky beyond belief.

The official handbook for the Old English Sheepdog says Boswell's breed "retains a puppy-like nature forever." I find this less than heartening. We got Boswell when he was eight weeks old. That was three months ago. When I think what the next 12-14 years might be like, I wonder why we didn't just stick with cats.

The answer to that, of course, is that cats don't play. And Bo, our son, needed something to play with.

At least that's what his mother, who on occasion claims to be my wife, thought.

"A little boy should grow up with a dog," she said.

Put in that context it was impossible for me to argue. I was once a little boy. And I grew up with a dog. He was an Irish Setter named Mike.

We lived in the country and kept chickens and one day a cantankerous, old rooster chased me into the house, pecking at the seat of my pants the whole way. I cried for hours.

I woke up the next morning to the sound of my mother screaming. Mike was sitting by the back door. The rooster lay in several pieces around him. Mike was a great dog.

And I'm sure Boswell will be a great dog, too.

In time.

Meanwhile he is living up to his name, or at least his initials. His complete title is Sir Oliver Boswell. You can figure out his initials. Let's just say I use them quite often when I need to get his attention.

Like when he strolls into the bathroom, takes the toilet paper between his teeth, unrolls it to its full length and decorates the house with double-ply.

Or when he gets to my favorite magazine before I do, thereby reducing me to the task of completing a jigsaw puzzle before I can enjoy my reading.

Or when he leaps into the car at the precise instant I finish washing the windows and demonstrates the latest techniques in smearing glass with his nose.

Or when he bounds outside unleashed and in a matter of seconds uproots two crotons, three schefflera and an entire bed of sprengeri fern, plants, I might add, that have taken me an entire year to grow.

But I am trying to understand these social statements of his. I think it speaks highly of my abiding tolerance and patience that I allow Boswell such free expression.

He walked into my den just a moment ago. First, he sniffed around. Then he just sat and looked at me awhile. He cocked his head to one side, as if he was trying to figure me out, too.

Now he's curled up around my feet. And — imagine this— he is licking my toes.

I don't know what kind of social statement this is either.

But I think I kind of like it.

Taking The Mullet Cure

"I've never met a mullet that I didn't like."

— Drew Lee Bonkers

Today's column is written in honor of Brevard County Sheriff Jake Miller. Sheriff Miller has devised a plan that could very well solve the nagging social problem of how to successfully rehabilitate hardened criminals.

It all has to do with mullet.

Anyone with a lick of sense who likes to eat good food knows about mullet. Especially, poor folks. For $5 a poor man can buy enough mullet to feed his wife, his kids, his neighbors and still have plenty left over to give his dogs. And everyone will love him for it.

But for those of you who are ignorant about mullet, first let me extend my sympathy, then let me educate you.

Mullet are fish. They jump a lot— a lazy, flat, floating leap that is a joy to watch. Old-timers call them "hardheads" or "fatbacks." They are totally unlike any other fish in this world.

That's mainly because mullet are primarily vegetarians. Other fish will strike at a piece of cut bait on a hook. But mullet have gizzards like chickens and mostly eat grass and weeds and certain kinds of algae.

Most people catch mullet with nets. And that's what Sheriff Miller hopes prisoners in the Brevard County Jail will soon be doing.

Sheriff Miller plans to start a "Mullet Patrol." Prisoners will go out on the Indian River, spread their nets and wait for the mullet to fill them up. Then they'll clean the fish, haul them back to the jail and all the prisoners will sit down to some good grub.

Sheriff Miller says he expects to provide his 300 or so inmates with two mullet dinners a week, thereby saving taxpayers some $15,600 a year.

What Sheriff Miller doesn't mention, but no doubt realizes because he is a devoted mullet-lover himself, is that this wonderful fish is blessed with miraculous powers that are worth untold millions of dollars.

Simply put, if you eat mullet it will cure your ills. Mullet will soothe your soul. Mullet will succeed where so-called rehabilitative experts have failed in setting criminals on the path to a righteous life.

I will call on Woody Summerall to explain. Woody works at the City Fish Market in Fort Myers, a noble establishment if ever there was one. He has cleaned millions of mullet over the past 45 years and also takes time out every now and then to eat a few. Woody is, to say the least, an authority on the subject.

"You can't go wrong with mullet," Woody says. "Smoke 'em, fry 'em, any way you want to eat 'em is just fine. They always do you right. They never let you down."

I would like to testify to this truth, too.

Not long ago, I was filled with ill-will towards the world. I won't go into details, but thanks to certain events I was foul of mood and close to committing any number of crimes that could have landed me in jail.

But a friend of mine by the name of Karl Futch called and told me that if I came to visit him he would take me to the finest restaurant in all of Florida. I went by Karl's office in Port Charlotte and we got in his car and drove around for awhile until we came to an old wood-frame house not far from the banks of the Peace River.

I told Karl it sure didn't look like any restaurant I'd ever seen. He just laughed and told me to follow him inside.

And there in the kitchen was Nellie Futch, Karl's mother, 75-years-old and up to her elbows in mullet that her son had hauled from the river.

"You boys sit down," Nellie said. "Everything's ready to eat."

And eat we did. Nellie put out a bowlful of grits and sweet cornbread and sliced tomatoes and watermelon rind pickles and a bottomless pitcher of iced tea. But best of all was the mullet, a heaping platter of it, fried in corn meal and looking so good that it almost made me cry just to see it.

Nellie set out some limes and we squeezed them on the fish and I am not one bit ashamed to admit that I ate so many pieces of mullet that it's a wonder that I didn't sprout gills and swim home.

All I know is that no sooner had that mullet hit my stomach than things seemed right with the world. I had been saved by the mullet cure. I could no more cause harm to my fellow man than I could scratch my butt with my elbow.

That's why I am pleased to hear that the prisoners in Brevard County will soon be eating mullet regularly. They'll be out on parole for good behavior in no time, model citizens all.

Then all we'll have to do is get mullet on the menus in Moscow and maybe sneak a little into the White House and the U.S. Capitol dining rooms. Once it gets digested all will, indeed, be right with the world.

Turner T.'s Thanksgiving Day Blessing

I understand that in heaven you have Thanksgiving dinner every day. If so, Turner T. is plenty busy.

I'm pretty easy to please when it comes to Thanksgiving traditions.

Doesn't matter to me whether I'm served turkey or ham, mashed potatoes or yams, oyster dressing or corn stuffing, pecan pie or pumpkin. I'll take whatever comes my way and enjoy it just fine, thank you.

The only thing I require at Thanksgiving, indeed, the only thing I demand, is a decent blessing before all the eating begins.

Now, I'm quick to admit that around my house when it comes to saying the blessing over everyday meals it's a slap-dash affair muttered by rote if at all. But I make up for it on Thanksgiving. On Thanksgiving I try to give one humdinger of a blessing, a blessing that would do Turner T. Watson proud.

Back before I landed this swell job as a newspaper columnist, I used to do some now-and-then work for Turner T. He owned a farm outside of Gainesville where, with his wife, Coreena, he raised cattle and corn and fixed up old cars and sold them for a profit. I met him when I bought a sweet little 1965 VW bug that I couldn't quite afford. Turner T. let me settle the balance by doing some work around his place.

After that, Turner T. would call me whenever he needed help digging post holes or hauling lumber or putting paint on his house or doing just about any kind of hard labor that a 70-year-old man should not be expected to do. I kind of suspect Turner T. actually would have preferred doing the jobs alone because that's just the kind of self-reliant and stubborn old man that he was. It was Coreena, I'm sure, who insisted that he call me to help out.

That was fine by me. I was going to college and beyond broke and glad to work for next to nothing. Truth was, I wouldn't have minded working for free simply because whenever Turner T.

and I finished a job, Coreena fixed us the kind of meal you could not buy in any restaurant with any amount of money.

I was particularly appreciative of these fine spreads since at the time I was existing mainly on black beans, yellow rice and white bread. While it is indeed possible to live on such a diet for an incredible length of time, I'm convinced that it's not at all worth it.

But back to Coreena's cooking. The woman knew her way around the kitchen. And when one year she saw fit to invite me by for Thanksgiving dinner, well, the haste with which I accepted was almost embarrassing.

I won't go into the calorific details of that memorable meal. You could get fat just reading about it. And I'm sure I was vigorously salivating when it came time for us to gather around the table and give thanks for our good fortune.

Whenever I'd eaten with Turner T. and Coreena before, Coreena had given the blessing, a short, simple verse that's familiar to everyone. It made good sense that she should do the honors, because she was the only one in the household who went to church or gave the outward signs of possessing what is commonly known as religion.

This is not to say that Turner T. was a heathen. The man had his beliefs, I'm certain, but he kept them well-guarded and I know for a fact that he hadn't been to church since his mother died some 10 years before.

So I was greatly surprised when it was Turner T., not Coreena, who offered the blessing that day. I don't remember his exact words, but I remember what he said. And, thinking hard about it, I can almost see Turner T. standing there, thick arms folded across his chest, more defiant than contrite, offering his Thanksgiving blessing.

"Lord," he began, "it's been a good year, like all the years before it and once again we are fortunate enough to share our table with a friend, which is a lot more than many others in this world can claim.

"Last year, Bill Collins and his wife, Virginia, sat down here with us and since then you've seen fit to take Bill from this world and into yours which has caused a lot of sorrow. But all our memories of Bill are good ones and for that we are thankful.

"It was a bad year for cattle and corn. The crop was good and the stock was healthy, but the prices weren't any better than in years before and the only way there'll be a profit is if I can sell some of these old junk cars around here to unsuspecting students from in at the university."

Turner T. grinned at me and continued.

"It's been a good year for fishing and while I haven't done worth a damn hunting I know those who have and I'm grateful on their behalf because it's not worth it listening to all their complaining when they haven't had any luck.

"Coreena and I have had our ups and downs like always, but, like always, they've worked out and I know she'll be pleased to hear that we will be going up to Birmingham to visit her sister for Christmas like she's been wanting after all."

If Coreena hadn't been the religious lady that she was, she would have interrupted the blessing right then and there and kissed Turner T.

"The kids are doing fine, although we don't see them near as much as we'd like to. Turner Jr. is working for that electric company out in California and his daughter Ruth is about ready to make me a great-granddaddy. Ellen is living over in Germany with her husband who's in the army, but they're due home next year. We miss 'em and love 'em.

"Finally, there've been some things going on in the world that I don't like and can't begin to understand, but all in all everything totals out good and I'll be back next year to settle up with you again. Amen. Let's eat. It looks good."

I guess I should tell you that Turner T. didn't make it back the next Thanksgiving to settle up again. One day during the early spring, he sat down after one of Coreena's fine meals, took a nap and never woke up. Coreena moved up to Birmingham not long afterwards.

So I'll say a few words in Turner T.'s behalf today before Thanksgiving dinner. Just like Turner T. said, there's some things going on in the world that I don't like and can't begin to understand, but all in all it totals out good.

And I hope I'll be back next year to settle up again.

The Flamingo Underground

Just before this book went to press it was discovered that agents of the Flamingo Undergound are trying to get our state song changed to "Way Down Upon the Cuyahoga River."

By now, most of you have probably read about the Great Plastic Pink Flamingo Caper in Quincy, Ill.

But just in case it slipped by you, here's a brief rundown.

It seems that a number of Quincy residents are disposed toward decorating their yards with plastic pink flamingos.

Now, it is not for us to question why they are possessed with this strange affliction, a malady that for some reason is peculiar to Midwesterners. We'll let the psychiatrists, who are no doubt studying the case, figure that out.

All we know is that while the good citizens of Quincy have been sleeping, someone has been stealing the plastic pink flamingos from their yards. Dozens have disappeared in the past few weeks.

A note, purportedly sent by the flamingo thief, claims the thefts were committed to point out the fact that the young people of Quincy are in dire need of entertainment and recreation. There is little else for them to do, the note says, but steal plastic pink flamingos.

So, police are calling the Great Plastic Pink Flamingo Caper a silly, teenage prank.

But I'm afraid the police have been duped.

Those of us who are more attuned to the facts realize that the note is a hoax and recognize this sorry deed for what it really is—yet another act of terrorism by the Flamingo Underground.

And sooner or later, those same plastic pink flamingos that were stolen from the lawns of Quincy will hit the black market and make their gaudy appearance in Florida, a state the Flamingo Underground seems intent on corrupting for its own base desires.

Little is actually known about the Flamingo Underground beyond the fact that it is a small, tightly-knit cadre of radical

Ohioans bent on turning the entire state of Florida into a Sunbelt Sandusky, a Tropical Toledo.

A recent investigation by this column has uncovered some chilling evidence which demonstrates that the Flamingo Underground's activities are even more extensive than previously believed. Among them:

- Agents of the Flamingo Underground, armed with cans of spray paint, recently invaded Daytona Beach and maliciously altered all public signs to read: Dayton Beach.
- Lobbyists for the Flamingo Underground have successfully infiltrated the Florida Legislature and convinced a majority of lawmakers to support a bill that will make it perfectly legal to drive smack dab down the middle of the road, go no faster than 15 mph in 55 mph zones and make sharp turns without warning in the face of oncoming traffic.
- Flamingo Underground agitators have enrolled as students at the University of Florida and appear to be succeeding in their attempt to re-name the school's athletic teams the "Fightin' Buckeyes."

But the most insidious of their plots, by far, is the infestation of Florida lawns with tacky plastic pink flamingos.

Through devious methods of propaganda, the Flamingo Underground has brainwashed thousands upon thousands of unwitting, Florida-bound retirees into believing that they simply must have at least one of the garish, fake birds in the yards of their new homes. The result— a hideous assault upon the natural beauty of this once-fair state.

But all is not lost.

A numer of brave and true Floridians, including myself, have banded together to form the "League Against Flamingo Fanaticism" (LAFF) an organization with the sole purpose of ridding the state of these plastic monstrosities and battling the Ohioanization of Florida on all fronts.

Although our resources are quite limited, LAFF has succeeded in buying up the entire stock of plastic pink flamingos at a number of discount stores and roadside tourist traps, disposing of the birds in public "flamingo burnings." More burnings are planned for the future and we will keep you posted.

But the Flamingo Underground has thwarted our efforts by stealing untold thousands of plastic pink flamingos from various northern locales— most recently, Quincy, Il.— and is now smuggling them into Florida.

So far, Florida law enforcement agencies have been notably lax in combatting the Flamingo Underground.

We at LAFF advocate a "Get Tough on Flamingoes" approach. We'd like to see police make regular rounds through the state's mobile home parks and retirement communities in search of the offending flamingos. Upon spotting one, the police would immediately yank it out of the ground and give it to LAFF for proper disposal. The owners of the plastic eyesores would then be turned over to a local LAFF-operated "Flamingo Rehabilitation Center" for treatment.

But until government officials come to their senses and get behind LAFF, we must rely on grassroots support if our goals are to be accomplished.

That means you brave and true Floridians must help us out. Be on the lookout for plastic pink flamingos and report them to your local LAFF coordinator. Then be prepared for the next public flamingo burning which will soon be announced.

In the meantime, join the "League Against Flamingo Fanaticism." And remember our motto: "Pink stinks."

The Amazing Eight Dollar Christmas Tree

It's not that I'm a cheapskate. But why spend big money on a Christmas tree when it would be better spent improving the quality of rum I can pour in my egg nog?

I didn't set out to buy the homeliest Christmas tree that ever existed. It just turned out that way.

It all started when I told the Christmas tree salesman I wanted something short and cheap.

"How short and how cheap?" he asked.

"Short enough so that it will fit on top of a small table in our living room, thereby making it impossible for the dog to chew on it, the kid to topple it over and the cats to use its stand as a litter tray," I explained. "And as far as cheap goes, well, let's just say it can't be cheap enough."

I followed the salesman across the lot. We passed some lovely trees, all bearing price tags that wouldn't look out of place on French champagne or Italian shoes. The farther we walked, the smaller the trees got. Finally, we stopped.

"Cheapest trees we've got," he said. "Go for $12."

He held up a few and I inspected them. They looked OK, but none of them really grabbed me. There are many things in this world I will pay $12 for, but a dead tree that sheds needles on my carpet is not one of them.

"Too big and too expensive," I told the salesman, "Guess I'll just go look somewhere else."

"Now, now. Don't be hasty," the salesman said. He was a Lion or an Optimist or a Rotarian or something and the tree proceeds went to a club charity. On the whole, I think these guys are nice enough, but a bit overzealous when it comes to fund raising. "There is this one tree — a nice, little tree."

And with that he rummaged around in the pile and pulled out a short, dumpy spruce, bearing a price tag that showed it had been marked down from $12 to $10.

"I'll give you $8," I said.

"Sold," said the salesman.

OK, I'll admit that I didn't give the tree a close examination. If a Lion or an Optimist or a Rotarian or something tells me it's a "nice, little tree," then I'll take him at his word. Besides, the price was right.

I took the tree home, put it in a bucket in the garage and called my wife to take a look at it.

The first thing she did was laugh. Then she looked like she would cry.

"It's so. . .so. . .sad," she said. "Hold it straight so I can get a better look."

It was while I tried to hold the tree straight that we came to discover that certain spruce trees —especially those costing $8 — can have curvature of the spine. In other words, there was no way I could make the tree stand straight. It had a vicious curve that started about halfway up, a curve that would make Fernando Valenzuela proud.

And something else.

I hadn't noticed it when the salesman was showing me the tree, probably because his hand was camouflaging the deformity, but near the top of the tree there was a gaping hole that contained no foliage whatsoever and then there was a little cluster of green at the pinnacle. You know how a poodle's tail looks when it has been shaved and groomed to leave a little ball on the end? That's the picture.

"I knew I should have gone with you to pick out the tree," said my wife. "What a lousy tree."

So we just let it sit around the garage for a couple of days. My wife kept mentioning something about how she was going to go out and buy a better one.

Then one evening, I caught her out in the garage looking at the tree.

"You know," she said. "I'd have felt kinda bad if this little thing was the only tree on the lot that didn't get sold and had to sit there all by itself on Christmas Day. I think it will look just fine once we get some ornaments on it."

We put it on a table in the corner of the living room and turned it so the curve points away from you as you stand in front of it. It still doesn't look anywhere near straight, but the deformity isn't displeasing.

In fact, once we got all the decorations on it, a wonderful transformation took place. What was once a short, dumpy $8 spruce turned into real Christmas tree.

I don't want to get sappy about this, but I think the whole beauty of a Christmas tree comes not from how much it cost, or how tall it is or how straight it stands, but in the way it makes you feel.

And sitting down in the living room the other night with my wife, watching the dog trying to chew the tree and the kid trying to topple it over and the cats trying to turn it into a litter tray, that short, dumpy $8 spruce made me feel just fine.

It's a good Christmas tree. Maybe even a great one.

Rally 'Round The Ol' Piano

Thanks to my boyhood piano lessons, I can still read music. Trouble is, I can't speak it.

Whenever I think about Christmas Eve, the first thought that comes to mind is of the piano in the living room of my parents' house.

It is a Steinway baby grand. My grandmother bought it back in the 1920s and installed it in the exact same place as it sits today. Nearly everything else in the house has been moved around since then, but not the piano.

I think this speaks highly of its steadfastness. I don't think it will ever be moved out of the living room. I hope not.

Of course, when the piano first arrived, the living room was called the "parlor." Like I said, this was in the 1920s. People referred to bathrooms as "lavatories" back then, too. It had something to do with culture and gentility.

My grandmother was very cultured and genteel. She no doubt bought the Steinway baby grand hoping that some of this culture and gentility would rub off on my father.

My grandmother had about as much luck in this as my mother had with me. My father and I both endured piano lessons. And we are both living examples of why parents should not waste good money teaching young boys to play musical instruments when such a thing as baseball exists.

Neither one of us can play the piano worth a darn. But we can sing like all get out. Especially when we've got someone good to accompany us on the keyboard, usually in the form of my mother or my sister, two ladies who can do things to "Oh Come All Ye Faithful" that you wouldn't think were possible. And I mean that as a compliment.

Every family has its traditions at Christmastime. In our family, the big deal comes on Christmas Eve, after dinner and before the midnight church service, when we gather in the living room to cut loose on Christmas carols.

It's part of the tradition that my mother and sister must be prodded before they will play for us.

"Oh, I've forgotten how to play all those songs," my mother will say.

"I haven't touched the piano since last Christmas Eve," my sister will say.

But this feigned reluctance passes quickly and before long they are pounding out the first bars of "God Rest Ye Merry Gentlemen" or "Hark, the Herald Angels Sing."

We've been doing this ever since I can remember. When we were kids, my two brothers, my sister and I used to dress up as Santa Claus and his elves and give a Christmas program for the rest of the family. One time, we even convinced my cultured and genteel grandmother, who must have been at least 90 years old at the time, to don a Beatles wig and a plastic ukulele and join in with us. It was a bit bizarre, but well-received.

Sooner or later, all of us kids passed through stages of disenchantment with this Christmas ritual. It's part of growing up, I guess.

There is photographic proof of my own disenchantment, taken during the Christmas when I was 17 and totally appalled at the cornball notion of standing around a piano singing Christmas carols with my family. The photographs show me sitting on the couch — a healthy distance from the squares at the piano— in my navy blue turtleneck and my black sunglasses, trying hard to look the cool Bohemian that I thought myself to be.

Fortunately, I only remained a jackass for a couple of years. Nowadays you'd have to rope and tie me to keep me away from that piano on Christmas Eve.

That's where I'll be tonight. We'll start off slow, letting my mother and sister get warmed up. But then my dad will chance one of his awful harmonies and my brothers will make up their own questionable lyrics to "Deck the Halls" and we'll sing our solos on "We Three Kings" and before long, if our voices hold out and the bowl of eggnog doesn't run dry, you'll be able to hear us all over hell and half of Georgia.

Singing "Oh, Come All Ye Faithful."

And "Gloria in Excelsis."

And "Joy to the World."

Indeed.

Taking The Buckeye Express

Lots of people thought I made this story up. I only wish I had.

It all started when I ran out of gas down in Bonita Springs last week. It still gives me the chills to think about what happened next.

But at least I'm here to tell about it and, in doing so, I will try my best not to make broad and sweeping generalizations about people from Ohio just because of a single incident.

Those of you who've read this column over the years, know I've been accused of treating Ohioans unfairly in the past. Now, heh-heh, I will admit to having had a certain amount of good, clean fun at the expense of the citizens of Ohio, but I don't think I've been unfair about it. Indeed, I've done my best to deal in facts when the subject at hand is Ohio.

For instance, it is a fact that in 1895 there were only two cars in the entire state of Ohio. They collided.

It is another fact that up until a couple of years ago Ohio license plates used to carry a nifty little slogan that read: "Seatbelts fastened?" This slogan was required by law, in order to give fair warning to motorists from other states where driving is a far gentler art. I don't know why they decided to remove it.

It is also a fact that I have had three automobile accidents in my life and two of them have been caused by known Ohioans.

With facts like this at my disposal I don't need to go making up lies.

But let's get back to the day I ran out of gas in Bonita Springs. I was a good mile from any gas station so I stuck out my thumb to hitch a ride. Wonder upon wonder, the first car by — a green Pinto bearing a blue and white Ohio license plate — stopped.

And friends, I mean it stopped. Smack dab in the middle of Bonita Beach Road it stopped, with nary a warning, causing a pickup truck full of construction workers to slam on its brakes and slide off onto the shoulder and a Toyota carrying a pretty lady to whip by on the other side, horn blaring, and the pretty lady shouting words you don't normally expect pretty ladies to shout.

It was quite a mess. Traffic stopped in both directions and everyone was honking and I hopped into the green Pinto and looked hard at the driver, an old fellow with a mangy stubble of beard and a grin that showed a mouth vacant of teeth.

"Howya doin,?" I asked.

"Oh, a little at a time," he chuckled. "What's the problem with all those cars out there?"

I started to tell him that some fool driver had just stopped smack dab in the middle of Bonita Beach Road, but I just shrugged.

"Sir," I said, "I need a ride to the nearest gas station, if you don't mind. Ran out of gas."

"Name's Fred. Ol' Fred. That's me," he said. "I'm 80-years-old and I've been down here exactly one month from Elmore, Ohio which is right between Fremont and Toledo, you know. Come down every year. Love it.'

I started to introduce myself, but I didn't have a chance because Ol' Fred wasn't about to stop talking.

"Used to work as a job foreman on construction sites around Sandusky. Did about everything. High-rises. Warehouses. Office buildings. Started off working a pile-driver then moved right on up..."

I noticed we were traveling at no more than 15 m.p.h. in a 45 m.p.h. zone and had just crawled by a gas station. But I didn't say anything until Ol' Fred, still yapping away, approached the second gas station showing no signs of stopping.

"Gas station there, Fred," I interrupted.

"So 'tis," said Fred. "Gulf. Where'd you say you were going?"

"I need some gas, Fred. I ran out, remember? Anywhere's fine."

And with that Fred whipped the Pinto in a vicious left turn and headed for the Gulf station. I'm sure he didn't see the Datsun that was headed straight toward us, the same Datsun that swerved to miss us and, in the process, knocked down a barricade alongside the highway. The barricade had been stationed alongside the highway so motorists wouldn't pull onto a new road that was in the process of being paved by the Gulf station, the same new road that Ol' Fred was now driving on while construction workers on all sides were waving their arms and yelling all kinds of terrible things about how Ol' Fred was ruining the grade they'd just worked so hard to smooth.

The construction foreman came up to Ol' Fred and was proceding to cuss him out good when Ol' Fred said: "Building a road here, huh? I used to build roads outside of Sandusky and..."

I stepped out, got my gas and snuck back out to the highway to hitch another ride to my car, but Ol' Fred spotted me and pulled right up.

"Young man, you didn't think I was going to leave you stranded did you? Hop in and I'll carry you back," he said.

Well, all I can say is that the return ride was worse than the first. Ol' Fred started off straddling the center line, which caused no little confusion to his fellow motorists, especially when a guy in a red car tried to pass us on the right, which scared the devil out of Ol' Fred who swung over to the right and ran the red car off the road. I closed my eyes when we approached the fellow on the bicycle. I don't know what happened. If we hit him, then it sure didn't make much noise.

"That's my car there, Fred," I said, pointing to the stranded Volkswagon.

"What's wrong with it?" asked Fred, as he turned another violent left in front of a Budweiser truck that skidded and swerved and somehow missed us.

"Outta gas, Fred," I said, holding up the gas can. "Thanks for the ride."

"Say, let me tell you about the time I was working in that machine shop outside of Sandusky," said Fred. He was still sitting smack dab in the middle of the road and the cars were honking like crazy.

I wanted to stick around and hear some more tales of Sandusky, but, gee, I had to run.

A Mixed Marriage Made In Heaven

This column is dedicated to Lysol, patron saint of the slovenly.

My wife is neatish. I'm not. People said a mixed marriage like ours wouldn't stand a chance.

"You come from different cultures," they said.

"You'll argue about your beliefs," they warned.

"And how will you raise the children?" they asked.

I'll admit, we've had our rough times. Indeed, there have been occasions when we both felt it would have been wiser if we'd heeded the advice of those who counseled us against such a marriage.

But, just like the old saying goes, love is blind. Thankfully, it has also played deaf and dumb as need be, too.

We weren't aware of our widely different backgrounds when we first met. Oh, I guess we each had our suspicions. It's difficult to hide your breeding. But by the time the issue surfaced, we were too deeply in love for it to really matter.

I had asked her to my apartment for dinner. I'd just sprayed the bug bomb and was searching desperately for some clean plates when she first broached the subject.

"I think there is something you should know about me," she said meekly, glancing about the place. "I'm neatish."

What was I supposed to say?

I almost sputtered forth that worn-out cliche: "Hey, some of my best friends are neatish."

But it would have been a lie. I didn't know anyone of the neatish persuasion. I'd only read about them.

"Does it really make any difference?" I asked, reaching out to embrace her.

"I'm afraid it might," she answered, wiping the smudges from her blouse.

She took me home to meet her family. They were rigidly Orthodox in their observance of neatish traditions. Beds were made first thing each morning. Dishes were washed immediately following every meal. The pantry was filled with all sorts of hallowed paraphernalia essential to the fulfillment of neatish ritual— Comet, Spic 'N Span, Tidy Bowl, Windex. Needless to say, it was all very foreign to me.

Her father took me aside for a man-to-man talk.

"You plan, of course, to convert," he said.

"No, sir," I said firmly. "With all due respect, I'm a practicing slob and plan to remain one."

There was a big scene after that. Lots of yelling. Lots of crying. But in the end we all agreed that true love was far more important than hygenic belief.

We had a neatish wedding. It didn't really matter to me. Besides, neatish weddings are much more fun. One thing for sure — it was the first time in my life I'd ever returned a rented tux without forfeiting the deposit.

I'll tell you the truth. Those first few months of marriage were hell. We each had a lot of adjustments to make.

Our first argument was over the vacuum cleaner. Now, I was willing to concede that the vacuum cleaner should, on occasion, actually be used. Say, four times a year, with the change of the seasons and only then if you've got white carpet.

She, on the other hand, had been brought up with the "Rite of the Daily Once-Over-Lightly," a ceremony she invariably conducted when I was comfortably stretched out on the floor and reading from one of my magazine piles.

One day the vacuum cleaner swallowed two pair of socks I'd been storing underneath the dinner table. I blew up at her. She started crying.

"If you just learned to put things in their place, then this wouldn't happen," she sobbed.

With talk like that I could tell she was getting hysterical.

"Now, now, honey, those socks were in their place," I said, seeking to comfort her. "You can never tell when you might be passing through the dining room and need a pair. Have to be prepared for emergencies. I won't mind if you try to vacuum around them from now on."

See how easy it can be when you're willing to meet each other halfway?

Since then we've been able to work our schedules out so that we each have an allotted time to devote to our beliefs. She has Saturdays to clean up all she wants. Sundays are mine for being a slob. The other days it's a stand-off.

As for the kid, well, we're going to let him decide for himself. Whatever he feels most comfortable with, you know.

But he does get a kick out of finding my socks under the dinner table. And I know for a fact that he has never used the vacuum cleaner.

Positively Negative Reinforcement

Whenever my dad used to paddle me he would say: "I'm doing this because I love you." Those words never took the sting out of a whipping, but I'm quite certain they helped it heal faster.

It has become the vogue these days for otherwise decent, well-meaning parents and school teachers to practice something called positive reinforcement.

Positive reinforcement is usually practiced on children and, in particular, those children who are inclined to misbehave. For reasons that should be abundantly clear, virtually all children are therefore eligible for this curious form of punishment.

In case you aren't familiar with psychological terms, positive reinforcement is a method of molding young minds into the habit of doing the right thing by offering praise rather than criticism.

Say your son comes home from school and, against your orders, starts sneaking Oreos from the cookie jar.

You say: "Son, if you don't stop sneaking Oreos, then you're going to grow up and become a thief and go to jail."

Then you give him a good spanking.

Now, the disciples of positive reinforcement frown on this sort of reaction. It can only do harm, they say, and if you keep it up, then your son will indeed become a thief and you will have to take his Oreos to the state penitentiary.

They would much rather you overlooked your child's transgression and concentrate on the positive side of his action. They would prefer you said something like: "My, son, but you certainly do a nice job of chewing cookies with your mouth closed." Or: "You sure did clean up nicely after you stole those cookies, son."

This way there is still the chance your son may become a thief, but at least he'll be confident of his good manners.

Being the keen observer of adolescent habits that I am, I can report that positive reinforcement is failing miserably. Children are not behaving one bit better today than they were nine or ten years ago when all this positive reinforcement business really got started.

Negative reinforcement works better for two reasons. First, it is capable of instilling fear and fear is a truly effective resource when used in conjunction with children. And second, by using the threat of bodily punishment, parents and teachers can enjoy a meaningful release that they won't find by mealy-mouthing cheerful statements that go against their true natures.

Please note that I say the "threat of bodily punishment." Actual whippings should be used sparingly and confined to those occasions when you can think of nothing threatening to say. This usually occurs when dealing with teenagers.

I can cite a perfect example of the effectiveness of negative reinforcement since it happened to involve me. At the time, I was 16, an age when I was highly impressionable and somewhat in need of the "threat of bodily punishment."

Also involved was a gentleman by the name of Ken Harsey, who, at the time, cruised the roads around my hometown of Leesburg for the Florida Highway Patrol. Patrolman Harsey later gained notoriety in Tallahassee when former Gov. Claude Kirk asked him to join his security force. Harsey was doing just fine until he told the governor's wife that her shoes looked like boats. He got fired. It made great headlines.

My incident with Patrolman Harsey took place on a Sunday afternoon. I had borrowed my dad's new pickup and was headed for some urgent rendezvous when I passed through an intersection and pulled onto U.S. 27. The fact that I ran the stop sign at the intersection is central to the theme of this story.

Well, a siren whined. A blue light flashed. I pulled over and Officer Harsey was soon stationed outside my door.

"Son," he began. "Did you see that stop sign back there?"

"Yessir," I said, for there was no doubt that I had seen it and no question but that I should add "sir" to my reply.

"Son," Officer Harsey continued. "What did you do when you saw that stop sign?"

"Well," I said, "I just kinda slowed down a little bit."

Officer Harsey grinned the grin of a man who is holding your foot in a steel trap and is prepared to snap the spring.

"Son, if I was to take this club here," Officer Harsey said, tugging at the weapon on his belt, "and started beating hell out of you and you were to yell 'Stop! Stop!' would you want me to stop or just kinda slow down?"

The logic was not wasted on me.

"I'd want you to stop," I answered.

"That's right," growled Harsey. "And that's why I just know you are going to stop from now on whenever you see one of those little red signs. Now get out of here."

To this day I cannot approach a stop sign without thinking of

Harsey and his club. This may or may not be a healthy response, but his lesson darn sure worked. Positively.

The Same Old Bunk

What we really need are politicians who are smart enough to realize that holding public office is such a lousy job that they ought to just forget it.

I get a big kick out of reading the paper these days. It's filled with stories about politicians running for public office.

Running for public office is much like declaring war. Only it's political war, the war in which everyone shoots from the lip.

You've heard the old saying that politicians make strange bedfellows. It's true, of course. What's more, they all share the same old bunk.

To prove it, all you have to do is listen to a politician make a speech. This time of year the air is full of political speeches. Trouble is, the opposite holds true.

As an exercise in vacuousness, let's examine the typical political speech, the speech that most every candidate seems to be making this year.

This speech generally starts with the candidate promising to take a "common sense approach to government."

Does this really mean anything?

Before an operation, does it encourage you for the brain surgeon to say: "I'm going to use a common sense approach in cracking your skull open."

When your airplane lifts off from the runway, does it put you at ease to hear the pilot announce: "Now, don't worry. This time I'm going to take a common sense approach to make sure we don't crash and die."

Apparently politicians are the only people who feel they must assure us of their common sense. This is because, once elected, they often demonstrate a notable lack of it.

A recent trend in political speeches seems to require candidates to promise they will "run government like a business."

Whenever I hear this I want to ask: "Exactly what kind of business?"

There are all kinds of businesses. A shade-tree mechanic runs a business. A loan shark runs a business. So does a child pornographer.

Are these the kind of businesses the politicians are talking about?

Besides, as everyone will tell you, business is not particularly good these days. There have been more bankruptcies in the last year than ever before.

Given these circumstances, maybe it's time we explored the notion of running a government like a government. As far as I know, it's never been done before.

Then there are taxes. No political speech is complete without a line about "cutting back taxes."

Now, there is absolutely nothing wrong with "cutting back taxes." But who in the world isn't in favor of it?

Politicians who say they favor "cutting back taxes," might just as well be saying they favor "breathing oxygen" or "eating food" or "getting a good night's sleep."

Let's not forget the old "it's time for a change" routine. As far as government goes, I think it's fair to say that it's always time for a change. Still, give me a candidate who has the guts to say, "It's time for the same old thing," and I'd vote for him just because he's given us a change in the same old political speech.

And there is always a part in the speech wherein the candidates promise to be "full-time" office holders, meaning they will devote all their waking hours to carrying out the duties of their elected positions.

I think one of the problems with government these days is that there are too many "full-time" office holders. There really isn't enough legitimate work for elected officials to do to keep them busy on a "full-time" basis.

A case in point is the city council that just spent several hours of its time debating whether the mayor should get new stationery. All too often, this is the kind of work that gets done when you have "full-time" office holders.

I'll take a part-timer any day, a part-timer like Thomas Jefferson, for instance, who gave a little time to being president and a little time to thinking up inventions and a little time to running the plantation. Somehow the country survived.

But then, Thomas Jefferson wasn't a politician. He was a statesman.

And a statesmen is just a politician who has been dead for a long time. We could use more of them.

Please, Don't Ask Me

The effect of this column wasn't as immediate as I would have liked. Still, 36 hours after it appeared we were celebrating.

I have just finished making a small sign. I plan to pin the small sign to my shirt and wear it wherever I go.

The small sign says: "Nothing yet."

I will wear the small sign because I am bound to meet a friend who will ask: "Any news?"

Then I am bound to meet another friend who will ask: "What's the word?"

And I am bound to meet yet another friend who will just ask: "Well?"

By wearing the small sign that says "Nothing yet" I can save us all some time.

Don't get me wrong. I appreciate the concern of my friends. Their abiding good will is most welcome.

It's not that I'm getting tired of answering their questions, it's just that . . . well, yes, I AM getting tired of answering their questions.

And if I'm getting tired of answering their questions, I can just imagine how tired my wife is getting of answering my questions.

"How do you feel?" I asked her when we woke up this morning.

"Just fine," she said for the umpteenth morning in a row.

"I mean, do you feel. . . anything?" I asked.

"No," she said.

"You don't feel. . . anything?"

"No, I don't feel anything and I just wish you'd stop asking me all the time."

I don't blame her for snapping at me. If put in her position I would have lost all patience long ago. That she remains even moderately pleasant in the face of all this impresses me no end.

The situation is this: The baby was supposed to have arrived 10 days ago.

You know how babies are. What's 10 days when you've been

lounging around for nine months? The baby will get here sooner or later.

In the meantime, our life is just not as it should be. It's a lot like an extra-inning baseball game with both pitchers throwing no-hitters.

The doctor assures us that there is nothing to worry about.

"Now, you know you can't rush this," she says. "Just take advantage of all the extra time you have now. Before long you'll be changing diapers and waking up in the middle of the night. Enjoy yourselves while you can."

I've tried, but truth is, I'm just not thinking straight.

When I left for the office the other morning, my wife asked me to drop off the dog at the vet's. I loaded the dog in the car and drove off, my thoughts on the baby that is overdue.

When I got out of the car at the office I looked in the back seat and thought: "Just what is the dog doing back there?"

On the return trip, I overshot the vet's and was pulling in the driveway of my house when I thought: "Just what am I doing here?"

Somehow the dog made it to the vet's and I made it to the office and that's the way things have been going lately.

We thought something was about to happen the other night. Debbie was in the bathroom, brushing her teeth, when I heard her groan and say: "I think it's starting."

So I opened the garage door and made sure the car was ready. I checked the camera and made sure it had film. I called my mother-in-law and made sure she was ready to look after our son. I drank some coffee and made sure I was ready to stay awake for awhile.

Then we sat and waited. The pains went away after a couple of hours.

Unfortunately, the coffee didn't. I stayed up for the rest of the night.

We didn't sit around waiting for our first child to be born. He just kind of snuck up on us.

We'd gone out for dinner at a fancy restuarant and were sitting in the cocktail lounge waiting for a table when Debbie said: "I gotta go. It's happening." And then she ran to the car.

I rushed up to the bar and fairly shouted: "My wife is in labor! How much do I owe you?"

The bartender said: "It's on the house. Get out of here."

I thought that was a pretty good deal. Consequently, my wife and I have been going out to dinner a lot lately, hoping for a repeat performance. This time I'd like to complete the entire meal before she goes into labor and let the restaurant kindly pick up that tab.

But so far, it hasn't worked. And our plan is getting rather expensive.

Someone suggested that if I started writing a column about how the baby hasn't been born yet, then surely something would happen.

Well, here it is.

I'm finished.

And. . . nothing yet.

The Facts About Dash

If my editor didn't watch over me, I'd be writing columns about Dash and Bo at every chance I could find.

These are the vital statistics:

Date of birth— July 26, 1982 at 9:35 p.m.

Place of birth— Lee Memorial Hospital

Length— 19 ¾ inches

Weight— 8 pounds 7 ½ ounces

Hair— Brown

Eyes— Brown

Parents— Bob and Debbie Morris

But vital statistics are just bare facts. They don't tell all you should know about Dashiell MacDonald Morris.

They don't tell about his cry, which is described on the hospital report as "lusty." And lusty it is, indeed. It is also loud and long-lasting and loaded with anger if it happens that he doesn't get fed on time. The kid has spunk.

The vital statistics don't tell you about his hands, hands that are remarkably large for one who is so small.

"Aristocratic hands," my father called them. "Just like mine."

But you know how grandparents are. Each one looks for something of themself in the child. And so far, each one involved with this child has found a little something.

All I know is that those hands, so soft and yet so strong, squeeze 'round my fingers and don't let go. I don't mind a bit.

And then there is his grin. The vital statistics don't tell you about that either.

Of course, some folks claim that a baby just barely a week old couldn't possibly be grinning already.

"It's just gas," they say. "It's gas that makes them grin."

I'll argue with them over that. Just a few minutes ago I tiptoed up to his crib and tickled him on the chin. He grinned. So don't tell me it was gas.

I guess I should explain his name— Dashiell MacDonald Morris. It's a name that has had lots of people guessing as to where it came from.

"How did you ever come up with a name like Dashiell?" I've been asked too many times to count.

I tell people that Debbie and I wanted our son to have a name with eight letters so we just started drawing out of the pile from a Scrabble game and Dashiell is what we came up with.

But that's not the truth. Truth is, I've always been a fan of Dashiell Hammett, the great writer of detective stories. He wrote "The Maltese Falcon" and "The Thin Man," just to name a few.

As for MacDonald, well, we just thought it sounded good. And it's simply coincidence that it's the last name of two other great writers of detective stories— John D. and Ross MacDonald.

So that's where Dashiell MacDonald came from. But we just call him Dash.

"Now, if you ever have a little girl, then you can call her Dorothy," a friend suggested. "Dot for short. Dot and Dash. Get it?"

Yeah, I get it. But there's no other child in the works.

Bo, our oldest son, is 16 months old and going strong. Dash shows every sign of keeping up with the pace. Debbie and I will be plenty busy for a long while to come.

We spent the previous few months telling Bo about the baby that would soon arrive. I would pat Debbie's stomach and say: "That's where the baby is."

At first, Bo would take a look at Debbie's stomach and say: "Ball!" After all, that's what her stomach did resemble.

But he soon got with the program. Sometimes at night, just before we put him to bed, Bo would crawl up, rest his head on Debbie's stomach and, in a real soft voice, a voice, quite frankly, that's unusual for him, he'd say, "Baby" and then kiss his mother's stomach.

In fact, at this very moment, Bo is sitting on the bed right next to Dash. He just leaned over, patted his little brother on the head and gave him a kiss.

I don't think I've ever seen a sweeter sight.

And, if you'll excuse me, I think I'll join them.

The Curse Of Good Manners

When it comes to salesmen, there's only one way to spell relief: R-U-D-E-N-E-S-S.

I was raised to have nice manners. My parents taught me that a gentleman always listens politely to what other people have to say and never interrupts or answers rudely.

I'm not about to suggest that I've been a total success in the field of manners, but I've tried to be true to my upbringing and I do pride myself in displaying certain courtesies to others, especially in matters of conversation. If someone engages me in a dialogue, I try to hold up my end with civility, understanding and good humor.

I think this goes a long way toward explaining why I am a failure when it comes to dealing with unsolicited salesmen.

Specifically, I am talking about salesmen who call me up at home. I just finished speaking with one a few minutes ago, hence the inspiration for this column.

This particular salesman was trying to get me to buy a life insurance policy from his company. I've been getting a lot of calls from life insurance salesmen lately. At first, I thought they might know something I didn't know and, frankly, this sort of shook me up. But a friend who is familiar with this racket told me that I'm on their list because I became a father not long ago.

I'd been wondering why all these salesmen started off their pitches with something like:"Hey, congratulations on that fine son of yours."

When someone, even a life insurance salesman, brings up the subject of my son, I find it hard to get rid of him curtly and quickly. As a result, I've spent countless hours on the phone discussing the ins and outs of life insurance, even though I'm already covered and not in the market for more. And, being the nice, polite guy that I am, I've even gone so far as to set up appointments for salesmen to visit my home for in-depth presentations.

This is the curse of good manners. I can't bring myself to be rude and tell the salesman to go away and leave me alone. And I never think of the proper way to handle these people until I've finally said goodbye and hung up.

That's why I've spent a little time preparing myself for future calls from salesmen of all sorts. Here are a few sample conversations that I plan to use when the situation calls for it. If you, too, are possessed by politeness and need a mannerly way to get rid of solicitors, please feel free to use these examples.

Salesman:"I'd like to talk to you about life insurance, Mr. Morris."

Me:"Don't even bother to talk. I want a $1 million policy immediately. I'm so glad you called. I've been thinking a lot about life insurance since my last operation."

Salesman:"Operation?"

Me:"Yeah, I just had a kidney transplant. Before that they removed my left lung. Then there was that triple heart bypass. Doctors don't seem to know the problem. Some strange disease without a cure. They... Hello? Hello?"

Or:

Salesman:"I'd like to talk to you about life insurance, Mr. Morris."

Me:"Ah, life, that poses a pretty question indeed."

Salesman:"Excuse me?"

Me: Life! Such an enigma. What do you suppose is it's meaning?"

Salesman:"Well, uh, I really don't..."

Me:"An existentialist, huh? A rather dreary philosophy, if you don't mind my saying. I tend to be a positivist myself, although I am afflicted by twinges of cynicism from time to time."

Salesman:"Actually, I think..."

Me:"I think, therefore I am. Cogito ergo sum. Not a bad little philosophy, but a bit simplistic, don't you agree? Hello? Hello?"

Or:

Salesman:"I'd like to talk to you about the Police Benevolent Association Benefit next month, Mr. Morris. Can I count on you for a few tickets?"

Me:"Oh, heavens yes. I wouldn't miss it for the world. I've got the cutest little outfit I'm just dying to wear."

Salesman:"Uh, gee, that's just great. Now, will you be bringing someone?"

Me:"Oh my, of course, you silly goose. I don't go anywhere without Bruce. What a hunk."

Saleman:"Bruce, huh?"

Me:"You bet, sweetie. We might ask our hairdresser, Mr. Pierre, to come along,too. He's divine. Simply divine. Of course, he'd need an escort. Do you know any cute, single cops? Hello? Hello?"

Busting The Gray Gangsters

This column probably generated more response than any other column I've ever written. Some people actually took it for satire and thought I was kidding around about bringing law and order to mobile home parks. Can you believe it?

I'm glad to see that lawmen have finally begun to crack down on a dangerous group of criminals who've escaped punishment for far too long.

In general, I'm talking about old people. Retirees. The Geritol Generation. The Wrinkle Brigade.

Specifically, I'm talking about the Largo 8.

Maybe you've read about the Largo 8. If so, then I'm sure you share my pride in the brave officers of the law who did society a great favor recently by breaking up the Largo 8's little racket once and for all.

Just in case you haven't been following this shocking story, let me fill in the details.

It all took place at the Ranchero Village Mobile Home Park which is, of course, in Largo. That's where all the members of the Largo 8 live.

Now we all know that mobile home parks, especially mobile home parks that cater to shiftless retirees, are notable breeding grounds for crime. The places simply seethe with all sorts of undesirable characters. I mean, you've got retired schoolteachers and retired municipal employees and retired small businessmen and they're all living right alongside each other and hanging out together and sooner or later something ugly is just bound to happen.

Let us picture the Ranchero Village Mobile Home Park recreation hall on the day the Largo 8 members showed up for their dirty work. A more despicable den of iniquity is difficult to imagine.

There were probably a couple of indolent old ladies doing needlepoint. Someone was probably putting a suspicious notice on the bulletin board about an upcoming bingo game. And the place has long been a known location of pot-luck suppers.

It was in the midst of this criminal caldron that the Largo 8 set up a card table and began their regular poker game. You must realize that this wasn't a small potatoes affair. Why, players could bet as much as 40 cents.

But, heh-heh, unbeknownst to the Largo 8, two undercover policemen were watching from a nearby pool table, which was itself a site for God-knows-what kind of illegal activity.

The undercover policemen were very clever. The Largo 8 actually believed the policemen were children of park residents, since most of the residents, including the Largo 8, are in their 60s and 70s and could easily have children the age of two grown men. So successful was the ploy that the Largo 8 even asked the policemen to join them in a cookout. The policemen declined, which was probably smart because they may have been placing their lives in even greater danger if they'd been dining with 60 and 70-year-old men with beer and barbecue sauce in their bellies.

Anyway, after watching a sufficient number of 40-cent bets being made, the policemen swooped down and arrested the Largo 8 and hauled in all the loot on the table which amounted to $24.

Six members of the Largo 8 appeared in court the other day. Two of the gang members didn't show up. One was in the hospital for a heart ailment. The other was undergoing cataract surgery. These old people will do anything to sidestep justice.

I'm a bit disturbed that the judge didn't hit these hardened criminals with the maximum fine. They could have gone to jail for six months and paid $500. They got off with a piddling $75 fine apiece.

But at least it's a step in the right direction. And it should serve notice to other old thugs that this kind of lawlessness will not be tolerated in the state of Florida.

Let's not stop with busting up poker games. There are plenty of other examples of crimes by these gray gangsters.

What about bingo games? Who are these oldsters fooling when they say it's just harmless fun? Same thing with duplicate bridge games that feature a cash payoff for the winners. And no more friendly wagers on the outcome of a shuffleboard match.

Thousands of old people make a mockery of statutes prohibiting co-habitation by two people of the opposite sex without benefit of marriage. They shack up so their social security benefits won't be lowered. It's a welfare ripoff if I've ever heard of one.

And what about all those old codgers you see just sitting around on park benches doing nothing while the rest of us are forced to deal with the problems of inflation, high unemployment and unyielding interest rates? Let's put some teeth into our loitering laws. Clean 'em off the streets.

I could go on, but I think you get the picture.

And the next time you visit one of those mobile home parks, please, be on the lookout for trouble.

Stalking The Wild Pater Holidayus

Unfortunately, there are no signs that this beleaguered breed will ever become extinct.

I watched the station wagon pull into the parking lot of the fast-food restaurant and knew right away that its driver was just the person I'd been looking for, the person who would show me that summer is truly here.

He pried himself out of the car, slapping aside all the telltale trappings jammed within — ice chests, roadmaps, life rafts, sleeping bags — and stretched his cramped muscles as the heat rose from the asphalt skillet.

He wore a dull stare, not unlike that of a shell-shocked combat veteran and seemed totally oblivious to the three Tiny Creatures who hung from both arms and one leg and screamed with competitive intensities: "Sally called me a bad name, Daddy!" and "I lost my coloring book, Daddy!" and "I don't want to eat here, Daddy!"

Slowly, he dragged the Tiny Creatures into the restaurant while his wife kept her distance. At the counter the Tiny Creatures shouted: "I want a strawberry milkshake and no pickles on my hamburger, Daddy!" and "I want a chocolate shake and pickles and no mayonaisse on mine, Daddy!" and "I want a root beer and mayonaisse on mine, Daddy!"

I knew for sure what kind of fellow he was when he said to the girl behind the counter: "I'll take all the hamburgers plain and small Cokes" and then turned to the Tiny Creatures and patiently explained, "Shut up and eat what I give you!"

Ah yes, he was one of them, no doubt. A true harbinger of the summer season. Generic name: Pater holidayus. Or, as he's commonly known, the Vacation Daddy.

The Vacation Daddies are out in full force this summer. While their species has really only begun to thrive in the last quarter century with the emergence of the two-week paid vacation, pop-up campers and far-flung relatives with convertible sofas, the Vacation Daddy is believed to have existed through all ages.

The Roman scholar Thales had Vacation Daddies in mind when he wrote: "I have chosen not to become a father because I am fond of children."

Likewise, Samuel Butler, the 19th Century English writer, considered the plight of Vacation Daddies when he wrote: "Parents are the last people on earth who ought to have children."

Vacation Daddies employ a variety of schemes in coping with their dilemmas, but the most popular by far is the Vow of Silence. It was my experience, in younger years, to travel with a Vacation Daddy whose variation on the Vow of Silence theme was a game called "Let's See Who Can Be Quiet Until We Get To Where We're Going." The rules were quite simple. Those who said anything at all — including the Vacation Mommy — were eligible for a quick backhand from the Vacation Daddy, although the Vacation Mommy always escaped such punishment and usually received instead a glare that quite eloquently stated: "You're asking for it." The winners of the game were promised a dollar for their silence, but to my knowledge, never in the history of the game was there a winner.

Vacation Daddies also follow an ironclad domestic statute called "The Law of It's Always on the Wrong Side of the Road," which is typified by the following conversation:

Tiny Creature: "Daddy, I'm thirsty. Can we stop at that drive-in for a Coke?"

Vacation Daddy:"No, it's on the wrong side of the road."

Second Tiny Creature:"Daddy, I have to go to the bathroom. Can we stop at that drive-in across the road from that other drive-in?"

Vacation Daddy:"No, it's on the wrong side of the road."

Both Tiny Creatures at once loudly:"Why, Daddy, why?"

Vacation Daddy:"Because I say so, that's why."

As effective as this law is, the Tiny Creatures have been known to reduce Vacation Daddies to blithering protoplasm with a game of their own entitled "The How Much Longer Game." It goes like this:

Tiny Creature:"How much longer 'til we get there, Daddy?"

Vacation Daddy:"About four hours."

Tiny Creature: "How much longer is four hours, Daddy?"

Vacation Daddy:"About 200 miles."

Tiny Creature after pausing no more than 3.2 seconds:"How much longer now, Daddy? Huh, huh, huh?"

Vacation Daddy:" !"

I'm sure the Vacation Daddy I was watching fit the ravaged mold as he dealt with the Tiny Creatures at his table. One was conducting an experiment to determine how far ketchup would squirt from an aluminum packet that has been stepped upon. Another was attempting to balance three dill pickles on his nose. And the third was improving her accuracy with chunks of ice shot from a straw.

I know the brilliant insight that was passing through his mind as he herded them to the car. To wit: "Insanity is hereditary. You can catch it from your children."

Are You A Hunk?

The only time a woman told me I had nice buns was when I was working my way through college as a short order chef at a hamburger stand.

I'm just old-fashioned enough that I still get embarrassed whenever I hear women talking about men.

I don't mean women talking about men and what they do for a living or where they live or who they're married to or what kind of cars they drive.

I mean women talking about men as sex objects.

I stumbled into one of these conversations that other day.

"A real hunk," I heard one woman say.

"Great buns," said another.

"He could put his shoes under my bed any day," said a third.

They were talking about some guy by the name of Tom Selleck.

Now, all my information on Tom Selleck is second-hand, but from what I gather he is the star of a TV show called "Magnum P.I." Before that he was the pretty face in advertisements for Salem cigarettes.

One of the women showed me a picture of Tom Selleck. I'll admit, he's a right handsome fellow, but frankly, he reminds me of one of those guys you see in the back of supermarket magazines in advertisements promising "You, too, can be a male model."

Not that I've got anything against male models, mind you. I put them in the same category as male manicurists and male Avon Ladies. You can draw your own conclusions. This is a free country and a man can be whatever he wants to be.

Allow me to make one observation, however.

John "Duke" Wayne would not have been mistaken for a male model. Neither would Humphrey Bogart. Or Gary Cooper.

I rest my case.

And I told the women I thought Tom Selleck was a cream puff compared to these other guys. Just another pretty face.

That prompted some hollers on their part.

"Tom Selleck has a sensitivity that John Wayne never had," said one woman.

"Bogart didn't have the bod that Tom Selleck has," said another.

"Gary Cooper paid too much attention to his horse," said the third. "Tom Selleck knows what a woman likes."

Clearly, there's an important shift afoot regarding what women like in their menfolk. I'm not altogether sure that I particularly like this latest trend. Still, it's a force to be reckoned with.

Bearing that in mind, I have put together a little quiz for all you men to take if you'd like to find out if you've got what it takes to turn the head of today's woman.

Just pick the answer that best suits you.

1.What I like best about my bathroom is:

a.The padded toilet seat and the fine assortment of reading material.

b.My vanity mirror with all its lights.

2.Before I go out, I like a couple of splashes of:

a.Bourbon on the rocks.

b.Cologne behind the ears.

3.Fill in the blank: Calvin —

a.Coolidge

b.Klein

4.Sometimes I wake up at night and worry about:

a.Taxes, the economy and my job.

b.The high price of dry cleaning.

5.Fill in the blank: color —

a.blind

b.coordinated

6.Gentlemen...

a.prefer blondes.

b.'s Quarterly.

7.I spend a lot of time working:
a.to pay the bills.
b.out.
8.I'd give anything for a:
a.low interest mortgage.
b.cleft chin.
9.What this country needs is a good five-cent:
a.cigar.
b.permanent.
10.I feel most comfortable in:
a.my worn out jeans and sneakers.
b.anything by Pierre Cardin.

Give yourself one point for every time you chose "b" as an answer. Each "a" answer rates a zero.

If you scored between 1 and 10, then you may very well be a "hunk" and eligible for the "Larry Lavender School of Male Modeling." Just kindly do me the favor of not parking your buns next to me at my favorite bar.

And for all you zeroes, the beer's on me.

Diseases For Our Time

I'm happy about the high interest rates. Now we can finally use all those columns in the amortization tables that sat idle for so long.

I felt like I was coming down with something. I went to go see the doctor.

"What seems to be the problem?" the doctor asked.

"I'm feeling dizzy and out of sorts," I told him. "I've never felt like this before."

The doctor nodded.

"Do you own your own home?" he asked.

"Sure do," I said. "Just sold the old one and bought a new one a little while back."

"Stick out your checkbook," he said.

I stuck out my checkbook and the doctor began flipping through the transition register.

"Hmmm, interesting," he said.

"See anything, doc?"

"I think so," he said. "I see here that your old mortgage payment was $218 a month. Is that right?"

"Yep," I said. "Had a nice little eight percent loan that we assumed from the previous owner. Hated to give it up, but we had to move."

"You weren't experiencing any of these symptoms in your old home were you?"

"No. Felt fine then, doc. Just fine."

"And your new payment is, let me see here, $465 a month?"

"Well, no. That was the first month, but then it increased to $525. And if you notice the latest payment there, it's now up to $599."

"Hmmm, just as I thought," said the doctor. "You've got one of those new variable interest mortgages, don't you?"

"That's right. Started off at 12 percent, which wasn't too bad. Then the prime rate jumped and the bank bumped us up to 13 percent. Now it's heading toward 14 and ..."

My vision blurred. My head spun. I felt cold and clammy.

"...and according to the terms it could go as high as 17 percent. Which means our payments would be something like $780 and..."

Then I blacked out. The next thing I knew the doctor was passing an ammonia inhalant in front of my nose.

"There, there," said the doctor. "I'll fix you up. Seems to be a lot of this going around."

"What is it, doc?" I asked.

"I hate to tell you, but you've got 'variable interest vertigo'," he said.

"Omigod," I said. "Is it serious?"

"Well, it's potentially fatal, but I think we've caught this case early enough to prevent you from slipping into the next stage. That's when it gets ugly."

"What's the next stage?"

"It's called 'monthly payment mania,' " the doctor said. "It's marked by total hysteria and insolvency. The first signs usually appear when the victim starts spending more than the recommended 25 percent of his income on shelter. I have some patients who are shelling out 60-70 percent of their income in order to keep the bank happy. I'm afraid they've passed the point of no return."

"Funny," I said, "but I've never heard of these diseases before."

"Well, they're all relatively new," he said. "And so far, no one has come up with a cure. But you're pretty lucky. At least you own a home. There are plenty of people who are shut out of home ownership altogether. They've come down with 'terminal renter's syndrome.' "

"Sounds awful," I said.

"Oh, it's gruesome. Severe depression and despondency, progressing into chronic anxiety over never being able to latch onto a chunk of what was once the American Dream," the doctor said. "It's not a pretty sight, but it's not as bad as 'bullionitis.' "

"Bullionitis?"

"You remember a few months ago when gold was selling for upwards of $900 an ounce? There were a lot of people who actually bought it then, thinking it would go even higher," the doctor said. "Now it's sitting around $450 an ounce and, I'm telling you, there are some pretty sick people out there."

"I'm sorry to hear that," I said. "But frankly, I'm more concerned over what can be done for me. Give it to me straight, doc. Can I beat this 'variable interest vertigo?' "

"Well, you could sell your home and go back to renting, but then you'd be susceptible to 'terminal renter's syndrome,' " he said. "Is there any chance that you'll be getting a meaningful raise in your salary some time soon?"

"Ha! You gotta be kidding."

"Got any wealthy relatives that might die in the near future?"

"Nary a one."

"Then I'm afraid the treatment I have to prescribe for you is one that you won't like at all," the doctor said. "But it's your only hope if you want to pay your bills and live in the manner in which you'd like to be accustomed. And even then, I can't guarantee anything."

"Tell me what to do, doc," I said. "I have to have some relief."

"Take a second job," he said. "And call me in the morning."

The Class of '99

It's not surprising that college tuition is skyrocketing. Can you imagine how much money it takes just to feed Herschel Walker?

News item:"Recent surveys show the average yearly cost of an education at a state university is $6,000 with that figure expected to increase to $12,000 by the end of the decade."

A glimpse at the cost-efficient future...

Good morning to you, the applicants for admission to the Class of 1999.

On behalf of the faculty and management of Abundant Profit State University, Inc., I'd like to welcome you to this campus tour. We hope that upon the conclusion of your visit you will join us as partners in a proud tradition — the search for truth, knowledge and a guaranteed 20 percent return on investment each quarter.

Follow me now to that choice chunk of real estate once quaintly referred to as "The Commons." Years ago, in less solvent times, this was undeveloped terrain, a broad expanse of grass and trees that was an embarrassment to this proud institution. It was here that the non-productive students of that era lollygagged about, throwing Frisbees, playing guitars, discussing philosphy and, in general, totally ignoring the reality of the marketplace.

As you can see, all that has changed. The Mining and Drilling Department, Inc., a wholly-owned subsidiary, began its strip operations in the early 1980s and when all mineral resources have been depleted and windfall profits totally realized, the land will be filled in and turned over to the Agribusiness Department, Inc. for the production of soybeans and high-yield grain crops.

You will notice that a dozen or so trees still remain along the fringe of the mining operation. If, for some reason, you are possessed by a wild, atavistic urge to sit under a tree and read a book, contact the Student Activities Corp. You'll find the hourly rental fee quite reasonable.

Speaking of books, to your right is the Turnip Memorial

Library, named after the late B. Ludfrum Turnip, former head librarian and originator of the brilliant "Bucks from Books" program now followed by all major universities. Turnip's immortal words, "Who needs a million volumes anyway?" are engraved above the entrance. It was Turnip who systematically trimmed the library collection down to its current 500 volumes, predominantly paperback, by selling the wretched excess of rare books and first editions to various pulp recycling plants.

Admission to the library is $2.50 during regular hours; $5 during final examinations. While we're here you should go ahead and buy a Library Lottery ticket. Who knows? You might just win a peek at the Encyclopedia Brittanica.

Next to the library is the R.O.T.C. building, headquarters of our world-renowned Mercenary Unit. I'm afraid the building is rather empty this quarter. We lost a lot of the guys over in Angola, but they did manage to earn us $200 a day apiece plus expenses while they were there.

I'd like to point out that the ivy which once adorned the walls of the R.O.T.C. building and others on campus, has been removed. We felt it took up valuable, income-earning billboard space.

Now let's stroll over to the stadium, home of our pro football franchise, the Abundant Profit Bottom-Liners. We're quite proud of the fact that we're able to keep the stadium's 75,000 seats filled to capacity even on days when the Bottom-Liners aren't playing. As you're no doubt aware, all classes at A.P.S.U. are held in the stadium with students seeking a B.S. using the West Stands and B.A. candidates in the East Stands. The end zones, of course, are reserved for our graduate programs. We think you'll enjoy hearing your lectures over the stadium loudspeakers and seeing your exam grades light up on the scoreboard.

Those buildings to your left are the former student dormitories, now part of the Real Estate Department, Ltd. Current asking price is $95,000 for a one-bedroom studio model, with attractive four-year balloon financing available. Those of you who can't come up with the down payment can contact the nonprofit Campus Camping Office for cheap tent rentals and a free map of available vacant lots around town.

You're in luck today because you can witness our graduation ceremonies. The dignified man in the three-piece suit is our president, the Hon. Suzuki Yamaha Honda. Instead of the once-traditional passing out of diplomas, you will notice graduating seniors filing by President Suzuki and handing him official-looking documents. Those documents — signed, notarized and legitimized by State Statute 141.11 — entitle the university to 10 percent of the graduate's gross yearly income for as long as the graduate is employed.

That concludes our tour and I'd like to remind you that while this service was presented free of charge, it is customary to leave a small endowment in appreciation. Checks, Krugeraands and American Express accepted.

Dynamite Donnie Scores

This is a fine example of how love, or at least lust, can make the rest of the world invisible.

I was sitting at the counter of a favorite restaurant, working on a plate of fried mullet, mustard greens, black-eyes and corn bread when the young man walked in the door.

He sat down at the counter, two stools between us, and looked the place over. He was maybe 20 or 21 and he wore old boots, new Levis, a short-sleeved cowboy shirt and a cap that advertised "Great Dane" trucks.

He glanced over at me.

"Howya doin'?" he asked.

"Just fine," I said. "How you?"

He nodded and kept looking around. He stopped looking around when he spotted the waitress who was working our counter. He kept looking at her.

She was about the same age as the young man and pretty in a country-western sort of way— brown hair teased perhaps a bit too much, a little heavy on the make-up, but she wore her jeans just right and her t-shirt looked real fine. It said "Even cowgirls get the blues" in glittery letters.

She walked up to the young man and without really looking at him said: "Ready to order?"

He just kept looking at her. He was grinning a grin that wouldn't stop.

"Don't remember me, do you?" he said.

She looked up from her pad, gave him a quick inspection, then shook her head no. She started to smile, then stopped it short. In a restaurant that gets a lot of men off the road, she'd heard plenty of this stuff before.

"A month or so ago at the Robert E. Lee," he said. "You were with your sister. I bought y'all some drinks. Pina coladas. Remember?"

She stepped back and looked at him again.

"You from Tampa and drive a truck?" she asked.

"Yeah," he said. "Haul dynamite."

"Oh yeah," she nodded. "Dynamite. I remember."

"On my way down to Miami with a load. Just thought I'd stop in and say hi," he said.

"Oh," she said.

"You, uh, told me you worked here," he said. "I told you I'd stop here and have lunch the next time I was in town. Remember?"

"Not really," she said. But I could tell she did. I had a magazine and was pretending to read it. It's the best way to eavesdrop in these situations.

The waitress took the young man's order and when she turned to go I pointed to my ice tea for a refill. She came back a few minutes later with his bread and tea. She'd forgotten my refill.

"Don't 'spose I could buy you another Pina colada could I?" he asked.

She laughed, but didn't say anything.

"Just gonna be here tonight. Don't have nothing to do. Thought it might be nice," he said.

"I'm 'sposed to be getting engaged," she said.

"That's what you told me a month or so ago. That's why you wouldn't dance with me. Remember?"

"Yeah? Well, I'm 'sposed to be," she said, looking at the floor.

"Shoot," he said. "I'm 'sposed to be getting engaged three or four times. Hadn't ever done it."

"Your order's up," she said, turning away. I caught her eye and pointed at my empty glass.

I watched her walk back toward the kitchen. She stopped and whispered to another waitress. Then the other waitress stole a look at the young man and said something. They both laughed.

She came back with his food, but no ice tea for me. I reminded her, but as she started to hurry off the young man said: "Your sister can come, too."

"Can't," the waitress said. "She's out of town."

She turned to go again, but the young man said: "You don't even remember my name do you, Mary Ann?"

She stopped and rubbed her cheek. This time she didn't hold back her smile.

"Danny?" she said.

"Close. It's Donnie," he said. "Dynamite Donnie your sister called me. Remember?"

She shrugged.
"Anyway, I'll be at the Robert E. Lee around six if you want to," he said.
"Have to work 'til seven," she said.
That's when I got up, went to the cash register and paid my bill. I looked back and Mary Ann was leaning on the counter where I'd been sitting. She was laughing. Donnie was talking about something and was using his hands to explain.
I guess I really didn't need that ice tea anyway.

The Truth About Sports

This explains why I can never get real excited about the Olympic Games. Any "sports" without cheerleaders or seventh-inning stretches don't thrill me.

A friend called up the other day and asked if I'd like to drop by his house and watch the game.
"What game?" I asked.
Long silence. I think my friend assumed I'd been locked up in a closet.
"You know," he said. "The Sixers and the Lakers. They're playing tonight."
Anxious mental scramble on my part to figure out exactly who the Sixers and the Lakers are.
Definitely not a baseball team. Not a football team either.
That left basketball and hockey. I chanced it.
"Oh yeah," I said. "The big basketball game, right?"
"Yeah," my friend said. "You want to come watch it?"
"Gee, sorry," I said, "but I have to, uh, sort out the extra clothes hangers in my closet. Maybe another time, huh?"
But truth is, even if there is another time, I'll think of another excuse.
I am not a basketball fan. I find it hard to get excited about an

activity that deals an unfair advantage to certain individuals simply because they have a hormone imbalance that makes them grow taller than other people.

Besides, when it comes to sports, it takes everything I can manage to follow baseball and football. You could make a career out of studying baseball statistics alone. Lots of people have.

And— why kids ourselves— baseball and football are the only real sports. Everything else is mere recreation.

I suppose this attitude might incite protests from fans of the lesser pastimes, but allow me to say a few words about the other so-called "sports."

Golf: Golf is just a way to ruin an otherwise enjoyable walk. It was invented in Scotland as a form of capital punishment. Notice that "golf" spelled backwards is "flog" and this point is proven. The best thing about golf is the clubhouse and the game is popular in America only because many people require an excuse to sit down and drink.

Hockey: Lots of people complain about the brutality of hockey. But that doesn't bother me. There's good reason why hockey players get in so many fights. If you had to play a game which was that boring, then you'd fight, too, just to break the monotony. Besides, if God had really wanted people to play games on ice, then He would have made it a little softer.

Rugby:OK, if you enjoy hugging other men in short pants.

Tennis: Any organized activity that can make someone like John McEnroe a millionaire is suspicious.

Soccer: In soccer, you aren't supposed to touch the ball with your hands. This makes about as much sense as swinging at a Fernando Valenzuela screwball with your nose. In Europe, they have the nerve to call soccer "football." I favor a United Nations resolution outlawing this slander.

Marathon running: This all got started when some Greek guy ran 26 miles back to his village to bring word that the hometown army had won some big battle. Then the Greek guy promptly fell dead on the spot. You'd think that modern-day marathon runners would have learned something from that poor sucker.

Auto racing: Auto racing is to sport what changing the oil in your car is to open heart surgery.

Horse racing: The same thing, except it's all orchestrated by midgets. Horse racing is often called the "Sport of Kings." It should be remembered that kings have enjoyed other sports— feeding people to lions among them. They are all of equal merit.

Gymnastics: Here are some things you have to do in gymnastics: balance on a beam, vault over something that looks like a barrel, swing on some rings, hang from some bars. It is nothing more than a fancy obstacle course. If this is sport, then so is Marine boot camp.

A Prayer For What's Fair

Institutionalized prayer is much like institutionalized food — bland.

Last week, when President Reagan sent Congress his proposed Constitutional amendment to return prayer to public schools, I couldn't help but think of Eddie Lieberman.

Eddie Lieberman and I went to school together back when the first order of business each morning was to recite the Pledge of Allegiance and say the Lord's Prayer.

Eddie didn't have any problem with the Pledge of Allegiance. But with the Lord's Prayer it was different.

Eddie Lieberman is Jewish. And the Lord's Prayer is a decidedly Christian prayer.

Eddie and I were good friends. We still are for that matter. I went to his Bar Mitzvah. He used to drop by my house to help celebrate Christmas.

We sometimes talked about him being Jewish and me being Christian. Nothing heavy, mind you, but enough for me to learn that Jewish children certainly aren't brought up learning the Lord's Prayer.

So whenever it came time to say the Lord's Prayer at school, I would sometimes sneak a peek at Eddie. Sure enough, his head was bowed, his eyes were closed and his lips were moving. Just like the rest of us.

I always wondered about that, so I gave Eddie a call the other day, shortly after President Reagan unveiled his prayer amendment.

"Were you just faking the Lord's Prayer or were you really saying it?" I asked Eddie.

"Oh, I was really saying it," he told me. "I had to didn't I?"

No, I told him, he didn't have to. Even when prayer was allowed in public schools it was never mandatory, just like it wouldn't be mandatory under President Reagan's proposed amendment.

"Maybe it wasn't mandatory," Eddie said, "but don't you understand? I had to say it. When you're a kid in school the most important thing in the world is to be like everyone else. So I bowed my head and said the Lord's Prayer, just like I sang 'Jesus Loves Me' every morning back in the first grade. Can you honestly imagine a first grader telling his teacher and the rest of the class that he doesn't care to sing 'Jesus Loves Me?'"

That made me think of another kid who went to school with us. I think his name was Michael. I never got to know him well.

Michael transferred to our school from out of town. On his first day in class the teacher noticed he wasn't joining in on the Pledge of Allegiance. She asked him why.

Michael explained that he was a Jehovah's Witness and that members of his church don't say the Pledge of Allegiance. That was explanation enough for the teacher and not another word was said about it. But from that moment on, Michael was effectively ostracized by the rest of the class. Some kids made fun of him. He was different.

President Reagan's proposed prayer amendment is short and to the point: "Nothing in this Constitution shall be construed to prohibit individual or group prayer in public schools or other public institutions. No person shall be required by the United States or by any state to participate in prayer."

But there are a couple of big things wrong with it.

First of all, if the amendment is ratified, let's not kid ourselves about prayer in public schools being voluntary. Simply saying that it's voluntary cannot make it so. Peer pressure is more powerful than public policy.

The second thing that's wrong with the prayer amendment is this: It doesn't give us anything that we don't already have.

A lot of people have been making a lot of noise in recent years trying to get the prayer amendment on the books.

"Let us pray in our public schools!" they shout.

Fine, go ahead and pray. There is nothing stopping it.

When the Supreme Court ruled against prayer in public schools a few years ago, it didn't strike down an individual's right to pray. It simply said there should be no organized, institutionalized prayer in schools, such as saying the Lord's Prayer after the Pledge of Allegiance.

There is no law in this land that can prevent public school students from bowing their heads and praying at their desks or in the lunchroom or on the playground whenever they feel like it. And God help us if there ever should be such a law.

The Supreme Court made the right move when it protected that individual right to pray or not to pray. We don't need to change it.

I asked my friend Eddie what he thought about President Reagan's prayer amendment.

"I guess I'll just pray that Congress kills it," he told me.

Well said. I'm praying the same thing.

Getting Fat For America

I'm always looking for an excuse to overindulge. This is the best one I've found.

I ran into my buddy Cadwalder the other day.

Leave it to Cadwalder to always have some new scheme for making money.

We're all familiar with his nationwide chain of test tube baby parlors— Designer Genes. And who among us has not envied his success with "Rent-A-Haitian," which solved the never-ending search for good, cheap help before it ran into minor problems with those nagging involuntary servitude laws.

Leave it to Cadwalder to always have some new scheme for making big bucks.

"What is it this time, Cad?" I asked.

"Fat," he said.

"Fat? Oh, I get it. You're going to jump on the bandwagon with Richard Simmons and Elaine Powers and help people get into shape, right?"

"Au contraire, you short-sighted schmuck. The diet and exercise scam is a dead end. The tide is about to turn. People are already starting to miss those lost pounds and inches and I'm going to cash in on it. Fat, my friend, is where it's at."

"I suppose you've done substantial research into the future of fat?"

"Oh, of course. I've proved beyond doubt that America was much better off when it was a nation of fatties. Look back at the 1950s and 1960s when two out of three Americans were overweight. Did we have 18 percent interest rates? No way. Did we have rampant crime in our streets? Uh-uh. Did we have to watch the CBS Evening News with Dan Rather instead of Walter Cronkite? Never. Then all of a sudden people started dieting and exercising and the country began falling apart."

"You make it sound as if putting on pounds is an act of patriotism."

"More than that, friend. It's a matter of national defense. Just where do you think all that lost fat has been going?"

"I've got no idea. I always thought it just disappeared into, uh, thin air."

"This is no time for puns, saccharine-breath. Not when the Russians are stealing our lost fat and using it for their own evil ends."

"The Russians?"

"They're getting fatter by the second. Think about the newsclips you've seen of Russia. Ever notice any skinny Russians? No, not a chance. It's against the law to be skinny in Russia. You have to sit around eating potatoes and slurping borscht and drinking vodka and growing dumpier by the day. Just look at their leaders. Breshnev, Gromyko, Khruschev— fat slobs one and all."

"But why?"

"Because there's only so much fat to go around in this world— fat is a depletable resource— and the Russians are stockpiling it. As a nation, America is tragically underweight."

"Just what are the Russians going to do with all this fat?"

"They plan to destroy us, that's what. We've all heard speculation that the Russians are working on an anti-gravitational weapon. Well, my sources tell me they haven't quite perfected it to the point where it will overcome our country's present poundage, but if America keeps losing weight at its current rate, then it's only a matter of time. The Russians plan to zap the entire world with this anti-gravitational weapon and watch us float off into the ionosphere while they just sit there fat and happy."

"Are we all doomed?"

"Right now we're headed that way. By my calculations, the only groups of Americans who have sufficient fat protection are the wrestlers on Saturday afternoon television and 96.2 percent of our nation's law enforcement officers. The rest of us don't stand a chance."

"That's where you come in, right?"

"Exactly. The local 'Cadwalder Aerobic Eating Center' is scheduled to open next week. You just come in and start pigging out until you run out of breath. We guarantee you'll gain 10 pounds a week with us. Then for those who like a little wrinkle in this routine, there's 'Jazzersit.' We give you a comfortable chair, a set of stereo headphones and 12-course meals complete with wine and flaming desserts. If you're exceptionally serious about getting out of shape and don't want to waste precious calories on chewing, special intraveinous feedings can easily be arranged."

"Sign me up, Cadwalder."

"That's the spirit. Say, how about one of these chocolate eclairs?"

"Mmmmm. Can you spare two?"

"With pleasure. God Bless America."

The Terror of North Carolina

Speaking for myself, I always do just fine on North Carolina roads. Unless, of course, I've been sampling a bit too much of Jimmy Jeff's special beverage.

Hi there, folks. My name is Julie Jean Witherspoon. I live on that big curve in the road otherwise known as Howling Rock, North Carolina and I have persuaded Mr. Bob Morris to let me have his newspaper column today so's I could talk to you about a matter of great importance.

The matter of great importance is the future survival of the good people of North Carolina. Our fate is in the hands of y'all down there in Florida.

Now I have read some of Mr. Bob Morris's columns when he writes about Ohio drivers and how bad they are once they get to Florida.

I wouldn't know about that seeing's how I've only been to Florida once and that was on a quick overnight run down to LaBelle with my husband, Jimmy Jeff Witherspoon. Jimmy Jeff, he's in the beverage business and he was hauling a big batch down to one of his distributors along with some of our cheap North Carolina cigarettes and he asked me to come along for the ride and to monitor the "Fuzz-buster."

I didn't get to see much because Jimmy Jeff he likes to drive about 900 miles an hour and once we got to LaBelle we just unloaded, got our money and then haul-tailed home. All I remember about Florida was the two zillion bugs that splattered on our windshield and the umpteen dozen armadilloes that met their fates beneath Jimmy Jeff's 18-wheeler.

So I can't pass judgment on the problems y'all might have with Ohio drivers down in Florida.

All I know is that we've got problems with Florida drivers up here in North Carolina. Big problems.

Seems as soon as it starts getting hot down in Florida y'all pile in your cars and head up our way to look at the mountains and get cool again.

Don't get me wrong. We're glad to have you 'cause you bring lots of money and I have personally taken in my share of it at "Julie Jean's Apple Cider and Homemade Quilt Stand."

Trouble of it is, you Flatlanders can't seem to get the hang of our roads. You're used to roads like that Alligator Alley that stretches clear across Florida with nary a curve and the only time there's anything like a hill is when you drive over a gopher or something.

You get up here in the mountains and you just can't handle it. You poke along about three miles per hour and when you come to a curve you hug the middle of the road, afraid that you're gonna run off the side and go falling down the mountain.

Well, the only folks who run off the roads around here are us Hillbillies and that's only because we have to dodge you Flatlanders.

Why just last week Tater Dewberry was coming home from Asheville when he went to pass this Winnebago with Florida license plates that was creeping up the road like a sow on its way to the ham house. No sooner had Tater pulled alongside that Winnebago than he saw another one coming down the other side, hugging that white line and heading straight at him.

Tater gunned it and left the road doing about 90. He'd have tumbled clear down to Coon Holler if he hadn't soft-landed in that big pile of corn cobs Rufus Hollingsworth keeps alongside his outhouse.

And you Flatlanders will sometimes just stop in the middle of the road to look at the darndest things up here.

Other day I was driving up to Albino Bluff when I turned a corner and had to pump the brakes and skid onto the shoulder to keep from hitting about two dozen Florida cars that were stopped and comglomerated like the road was a parking lot. I got out of my car and walked up to this fellow with a camera around his neck and asked him what was going on.

"Just enjoying that beautiful waterfall," he said, pointing to the side of the mountain.

Shoot, I just got in my car and drove off. Didn't have the heart to tell those folks that the top of the mountain is where the Bulow brothers keep their hog pens and that beautiful waterfall was nothing more than the excess slop they have to drain off every now and then.

So, you folks do us a favor from now on. Soon as you cross that Georgia line and get into our North Carolina mountains, don't drive another inch. Walk yourself to the nearest phone booth and just give me, Julie Jean Witherspoon, a call.

I will see to it that my husband Jimmy Jeff or one of his associates comes down to meet you and personally chauffeurs you around our lovely neck of the woods. I guarantee you will have the ride of your lives and it won't cost you a cent.

'Course you will be making a stop at "Julie Jean's Apple Cider and Homemade Quilt Stand" where you are welcome to lighten your pockets of some of that good Florida money.

And Jimmy Jeff says that if you keep quiet about where you got it he just might sell you some of his famous beverage. Goes for $4 a pint and you can keep the Mason jar.

Why I'm A Married Man

My wife said this column was better than a dozen red roses. I didn't tell her, but it was a damn sight cheaper, too.

I came home late the other night. Matter of fact, it was real late. Truth is, it was early in the morning.

I crawled into bed and she said: "I missed you."

Not, "Where have you been?" Not, "Do you know what time it is?" Not, "Go sleep in the den."

But, "I missed you."

That's one reason why I love her.

There are plenty of other reasons.

For one thing, she is beautiful. I know it's corny, but I'll say it anyway: The beauty isn't just on the outside. It goes all the way to the bone.

When I met her, I knew right away I would marry her. There is a good story about that.

We'd been seeing each other for a month or so and I decided to take her on a camping trip. We got a canoe and went down the Peace River. Picked a fine place on a lovely bluff and set up camp. Came time to build a fire and we went looking for wood.

I was the first one to spot the deer's antler. It had been shed beside a stump— one-half of a rack, five points, a nice trophy. I carried it back to camp and she kept looking for wood.

She was gone for about an hour. I saw her coming from a long way off, but she wasn't carrying any firewood. She was holding the matching antler.

She'd found it half-a-mile away from the other one, just stumbled across it while stepping over a log.

The antlers matched up perfectly. We mounted them over the entrance to our tent. You better believe we still have them.

I like to think the whole thing was kind of symbolic. You can figure it out. I believe in fate and after the antlers I understood we were just fated to stick together.

I would like to emphasize that "stick together" part.

I will not say that it has been easy. It wouldn't be worth anything if it were easy. We've had some rough times, times when we've both said and done things that we've regretted later. I don't know of many marriages where that doesn't hold true.

But the past five years have been the best years of my life. I'm looking forward to the rest being even better. With her.

I could go on and on about what she does to make me love her. Since it's Valentine's Day, I think I will.

- She laughs a lot. Usually at me. I need that. Keeps me humble.
- She works hard. And again I am humbled. There is no way I can keep up with her.
- She cooks the best eggplant parmigiana I have ever eaten. The three-alarm chili, blueberry muffins and Key lime pies ain't bad either.
- She never complains when I don't take the time to put my dirty clothes in the hamper. Ditto when I do a lousy job on the dishes, forget to take out the garbage and neglect feeding the cats.
- She likes to argue. And she is good at it. I appreciate her spirit and congratulate her on the consistency with which she wins our debates. However, I'd like to remind her that it is still not the right time for new living room furniture. A boat comes first. She'll understand.
- She is a fine mother. There couldn't be a better one. I know our little boy agrees. And the baby that's due in July will be blessed with her undying devotion.
- She knows what I'm thinking without me having to say anything about it. This helps. Especially when she just comes up and puts her arms around me at times when I really need it.
- She can't give a back rub worth a darn, but she's a great snuggler.
- She pays all our bills on time. If it were left to me, the collection agency would be camped out on our front lawn.
- She knows how to dress up pretty. All the time. I have never seen anyone else look so pleasing in just a t-shirt and jeans. And what she does to a new dress you just wouldn't believe. Makes me think that maybe I ought to get her one.
- She tolerates my stinking cigars and my filthy spittoon. I try to compensate by putting up with her Barbra Streisand

albums and her ability to fritter away time taking care of "just one little last thing" before we get ready to go out.

- She knows better than to carry on a conversation with me when the shower is running.
- She is always there when I need her. You don't know how much that means to me.

Like I said, I could go on and on. But let's just end it with a Happy Valentine's Day, Debbie. I do love you.

A Cram Course In Science

If science is so damn advanced, then why can't we make razor blades that last a lifetime? Or prevent bathtub rings? Or cure snoring? Or recycle electricity? Or videotape dreams? Just answer me that.

I've just finished reading a newspaper story about how America is becoming a nation of math and science illiterates.

Compared to youngsters in other countries, especially Russia, American kids just aren't learning enough to survive in a complex technological world.

This means grave consequences for our nation's future economy and defense.

Or so the story says.

Here are some examples of how American kids are falling behind:

- The average American student takes one year of high school geometry. Russian students take 10 years.
- Fewer than one in 10 American students take a high school physics course. All the Russian kids take physics.
- Only 16 percent of our kids take a chemistry course. All Russian students must take four years of chemistry.

Let me make a few comments about those statistics.

Frankly, I think they are just further examples of how good

we've got it here in America, land of the free and home of the lay-away plan.

I would volunteer for a life term in the Siberian salt mines before I took one year of geometry. Faced with a mandatory 10 years of hypotenuses and Pythagorean theorem, I would consider suicide, maybe by downing a gallon of Russian vodka and chasing it with a reading from Marx or listening to Radio Moscow. Enough to kill anyone.

I took high school physics. Here's the kind of problem you are asked to solve in high school physics: A two-pound brick falls off the roof of a 12-story department store. How fast is the brick going when it strikes the pavement and on which floor will you find the lingerie department?

The formula you use to figure that out is something like xy1824 ft. per sec. X 36D cup.

As far as chemistry goes, I can't say enough good things about that subject, seeing as how it got me where I am today. I took four years of chemistry, just like the Russian students. Trouble is, it was chemistry 101 for four straight years. After the fourth "F" I dropped out of school and started my brilliant career in journalism. So let's hear it for chemistry.

Still, I am a bit disturbed that we might be falling behind the Russians. I feel it is my patriotic chore to do something about it. That's why I have come up with this cram course in math and science.

Please study it. This is everything you need to know.

Basic Math: Pete Rose comes to bat four times in the first baseball game of the season. He gets three hits. Divide four into three and you will discover that Pete Rose is batting .750 for the season. Russian kids would be lost with a problem like this.

Advanced Math: You need $10,000 in a hurry. Frankie the Shyster gives it to you and says the 60 percent interest is due next Friday if you know what's good for you. To find out how much you owe Frankie the Shyster, go to the discount store, pay $7.95 for a Texas Instruments calculator and let the damn machine figure it out. Then leave town. Russian kids don't have discount stores and even if they did they could never get their hands on the $7.95 for a calculator. And they would never have the pleasure of dealing with a hero of capitalism like Frankie the Shyster.

Basic Chemistry: Here is a formula: 1.Pour 750 ml. of hydrochloric acid into a one liter beaker. 2. Stir it around with your finger. 3. Notice how much shorter your finger is. This should teach you better than to fool around with chemicals.

Advanced Chemistry: Here is another formula: 1.Take four ounces each of gin, bourbon, tequila, Mad Dog 20-20, sloe gin and anything else that might be laying around. 2. Mix it all in a big glass and swallow it as quickly as you can. 3. The next morning, go to your medicine cabinet and eat everything that looks as if it might help you out. Maybe you'll feel better, maybe you won't. Again, this should teach you better than to fool around with chemicals.

That should do it. As you might guess, I'm not too worried about the ability of our kids to survive in a complex technological world.

If it ever gets down to the nitty-gritty, I know our youngsters can whip those Russky brats in Space Invaders any day.

Passing The Torch Of Knowledge

I follow the Three B's of Speechmaking: Be introduced, Be Brief, Be seated. This one lasted a bare six minutes. That's why everyone applauded.

I don't care what some people say about the current crop of graduates from our public schools.

I happen to be quite impressed by them, mostly because one local class had the great wisdom and good taste to ask me to deliver their commencement speech.

Here's what I told them:

"This is the very first time I've ever been asked to give a commencement speech. I am deeply honored. I am flattered. And I thank for asking me to be here.

"But I must be candid with you. I have no earthly idea what I am supposed to say.

"Normally, when I give speeches around the community, I just tell a few funny stories. Then I answer some questions. And then I sit down. It's very easy. And it seems to work just fine.

"But from what I gather, that's not what you're supposed to do with a commencement speech. With a commencement speech, the speaker is obliged to be profound. He is obliged to be wise. He is obliged to dispense great and glorious insight as to what life is really all about.

"Please understand that I find it extremely difficult to deal with these obligations. I cannot meet them, not by a long shot.

"Under most circumstances, I am far more likely to be profane than profound, although I have cleaned up my act for this occasion due to these hallowed surroundings and this polite company.

"I cannot remember ever being called 'wise,' unless 'wise' was used in conjunction with the word 'guy' or another word that is somewhat coarse and does not bear repeating.

"And even if I did have great and glorious insight as to what life is really all about — which I don't— I'd be reluctant to dispense it, free of charge, to a bunch of people dressed up in bedspreads and wearing silly, little hats.

"So where does that leave us? Gee, I don't know. I guess it means you don't get a commencement speech.

"But believe me. That ain't all bad.

"Last night, when I was preparing for this, I thought back to my own high school commencement. And I'll tell you something. I can't remember a thing the speaker said. I can't even remember who the speaker was.

"I'm sure it's the same for your parents and teachers. No one really remembers what was said at their high school commencement speeches. Commencement speeches are highly forgettable.

"There is a reason for this, of course.

"You probably don't know this— in fact, I'm absolutely sure you don't know this— but until today, when you so kindly asked me to speak here, every commencement speaker throughout the course of history has belonged to a secret club. That's right, a secret club.

"As members of this secret club, they are all given copies of the exact same speech which they then deliver at all the commencements where they are asked to appear. The beauty of this speech is that upon hearing the very last word, everyone who has been forced to listen to it immediately forgets everything that was said.

"It just so happens that through my confidential sources I have obtained a small portion of this great, forgettable commencement speech. Allow me to share it with you:

" 'Ladies, gentlemen and graduates of fill in the blank:

" 'You embark today down the great highway of life. We have handed you the golden torch of knowledge. You are ready to set sail on the great sea of destiny. It will not always be a smooth voyage, but keep that golden torch of knowledge burning and you will not lose sight of your goals and if at first you don't succeed then try, try again.'

"I think you get the picture. You've heard all that stuff before.

"As you might expect, the great, forgettable commencement

speech does not come cheap. It costs big money to belong to this secret club and get a copy of the entire thing. That's the reason I'm not a member. We writers are a desperately poor lot and I couldn't even begin to scratch together the initiation fee, much less the yearly dues. So, I cannot read you the entire great, forgettable commencement speech.

"Sorry, but I'm afraid you are doomed to remember everything I have to say.

"But don't worry. I'm not going to say a lot more. I'm as anxious to get out of here as you are.

"The main reason commencement speakers stick to this tradition of telling you things that you immediately forget is that, quite frankly, there is nothing they can tell you that will really help you out. And there is nothing they should tell you.

"What this ceremony is all about is to let you know— to give you notice— that for better or worse you are ready to think for yourselves.

"Yes, just like that great, forgettable and dumb commencement speech says: You are about to embark down the great highway of life.

"Maybe you'll leave here and go to college. Maybe you'll get jobs. Maybe you'll get married and raise families. Maybe you'll be happy. Maybe you'll be sad. Maybe you'll find success. Maybe you'll find failures.

"But one thing for sure— no maybes about it— you'll find it all out for yourselves. It's all on you for the rest of the way.

"So I won't presume to tell you anything. It won't do any good.

"I will, however, ask you something. I will ask you a favor.

"This world is not a perfect place. There's a whole lot that's wrong with it. There's a whole lot that needs to be changed.

"Maybe you can make it better. And then again, maybe not.

"But, let's face it. This is the only world we've got. There aren't any alternatives. And all in all it's an OK place.

"Anyway, I kinda like it. I kinda like it a lot.

"So please, I ask you this one favor. Just don't do anything to mess the place up.

"Thank you and good luck."

Oh,
For A
Midnight Suicide

"It's too quiet in the back booth. Just what's going on?"
— Doc Carney

Every now and then — usually about 3 o'clock in the afternoon — I get the urge for a special beverage. If I'm in the vicinity of a place where there's hope these special beverages might be served, I'll go inside and order one.

"Gimme a vanilla Coke," I'll say.

"We don't make 'em," is the usual reply.

"What about a Cherry Smash?" I'll try again.

"We don't make them either," comes the answer, bearing signs of hopeless exasperation.

By this point, I realize it's a no-win situation. Still, I give it a final shot.

"What about a . . ." and I pause for dramatic effect. ". . . a Midnight Suicide?"

This is when the person behind the counter usually scowls and says something like: "Listen, we've got Coca-Cola, root beer, Tab or Seven-Up. Take your pick."

So much for my 3 p.m. pick-me-up.

If only Carney's Drug Store was still around. Doc Carney would have fixed me up with whatever I wanted, then let me sit around reading comic books and wasting time for the rest of the afternoon.

Carney's Drug Store was where I spent the better part of my youth, at least that crucial portion between the age of 10 and 16, when I was old enough to wander away from home but too young to drive a car. Carney's sat on Main Street in Leesburg, my hometown, conveniently located on my route home from school. It was on everyone's route, even if they lived clear across town.

That's because Carney's was sort of like a cocktail lounge for kids. Most everyone I knew raced straight there after school with hopes of getting first shot at the comic book rack and a seat in the infamous "Back Booth."

Doc Carney was a nice, old man who wore rimless spectacles

and bore an uncanny resemblance to Franklin Delano Roosevelt, especially when he was using his ivory cigarette holder. He wasn't a pharmacist and his place was a drug store by name alone. Oh, it carried a slew of patent medicines, toilet articles and a thorough selection of fishing tackle. But there was dust on all that stuff.

The only thing I ever saw anyone buy at Carney's was ice cream, homemade lemonade and Doc's specialty soft drinks. He never served pre-mixed drinks like most every place does these days. If you ordered a vanilla Coke it demanded four important steps. First, Doc had to chip ice off a big block and put the chunks into a paper cup. Next, he shot a healthy squirt of cola syrup onto the ice. And then a smidgen of vanilla. The final step was a splash of carbonated water from a big, stainless steel spigot.

If you were a real big spender, you plunked down an extra dime and ordered a Midnight Suicide. For the money, you got a little bit of everything that Doc's spigots would squirt. Cola, grape, orange, cherry, vanilla, chocolate . . . the works.

Of course, it took Doc a couple of minutes to make one of his special drinks, but the wait was worth it, not only for the drink itself, but because when you bought something you were entitled to take a seat and help yourself to the magazine rack. Unlike other drugstore owners, Doc never made kids buy comic books if they wanted to read them in his place. Whatever was in the rack was yours to flip through. I killed many an afternoon following the exploits of Superman, Batman and the rest of the super-heroes.

But the real adventures came in the "Back Booth," where the high side panels afforded occupants a bit of privacy. More than one love affair began— and ended— in the Back Booth. The walls of Carney's were testament to that. Doc let you write anything you wanted to on the wall as long as it wasn't dirty. Decades-old inscriptions reached to the ceilings, scrawled in lipstick, crayons and magic marker: "Lynne Luvs Tony," "Rick and Suzanne 4-ever" and "Michael Gray stinks."

Doc Carney died a few years back. His wife tried to run the drugstore for awhile, but it was too much for her. She sold the place and someone turned it into a pawn shop.

I was lamenting the disappearance of places like Carney's the other day in the presence of a 13-year-old acquaintance.

"No big deal," she said. "We've got convenience stores where we can hang out."

So I visited one of the convenience stores not far from a school in my neighborhood. Sure enough, a dozen or so kids stood lined up by the door. Inside, a couple of kids waited for the uniformed clerk to fill cups with a frozen concoction containing more air than anything else. The comic books were in a rack bearing the warning: "If you want to read it, buy it."

And on the door, where the kids were lined up, was the sign: "No more than three students allowed in this store at one time."
No, it wasn't at all like Carney's. It wasn't even close.

My Vote For Monolingualism

The only foreign language I'd really like to learn is the one spoken by the IRS.

Being the dollar-wise man that I am, I like to flip the pages of "Money" magazine every now and then.
Even though I don't have an extra $10,000 to stick away in high-yield bonds or even a lousy couple of hundred to play the penny stocks, I enjoy the vicarious sense of feeling flush that comes from reading the magazine. One day in the future, I keep telling myself, I will arrive at a station of financial solidity allowing me to actively engage in all the nifty little investment schemes that "Money" keeps telling me about. It is this hope for the future that keeps me going, however humbly, between paychecks.
But now, a recent issue of "Money" tells me, the future is no longer mine. The future, "Money" says, belongs to those nimble-tongued souls who can speak two languages. "In an era of ever-increasing international dependencies and world-wide commerce, the only individuals who can count on prosperity are those who have expanded their vocabularies beyond the limitations of a mother tongue," the article says. In other words, there are big bucks in store for the bilingual.
Which means I am definitely in for some lean years. If success will only come from the mastery of a foreign language, then I had best prepare myself for another decade of deficit spending.
Not that I haven't tried to improve myself in this field. Indeed, I have given foreign languages my best shot. The backfires have been notable.
It all began in high school when I took Latin, the most foreign

of all languages, unless of course, one happens to live in the Vatican. At the time I was entertaining thoughts of becoming a lawyer and Latin, the guidance counselor told me, was the modus operandi that would get me there, presenting me with all sorts of valuable basic skills along the way. The only valuable basic skill I got from Latin was one that enabled me to write the complete translation of Ceasar's Gallic War journals in miniature on the soles of my tennis shoes as my modus operandi for passing the final exam. The only place it got me, however, was the principal's office where I was given 10 swift swats and a fat "F" for the year. So long, summa cum laude.

Somehow I made it to college where, entertaining thoughts that I would become a biologist, I was counseled to take German. I made truly impressive grades, largely because my professor, an old man with the unlikely name of Dr. Bub, was deaf, blind and tenured. Whenever he called on me in class, I merely mumbled, but mumbled with great flourishes so that he thought I was actually speaking German. When it came time for exams, the basic skills learned in Latin really paid off since Dr. Bub couldn't see past the edge of his desk, much less all the way to the soles of my shoes.

I made such good grades in German that I even convinced myself I could speak the language, a delusion that proved disasterous when I happened to visit the Rhineland a few years back. Rushing through the streets of Munich one evening, late for my destination at the train station, I stopped to ask a nice-looking woman if she had the time.

I asked in my best German, complete with flourishes.

The next thing I knew she was slamming her pocketbook into my head and using words that I'm sure were never spoken in Dr. Bub's class. As I learned from a fluent friend a few days later, the German words I used did indeed mean "Have you the time?" But the phrase was common parlance for "Have you the time to dally around?" and was usually reserved for addressing ladies of a different occupation than the woman with the lethal pocketbook.

The last language I attempted was Arabic, when I was entertaining the notion of somehow entrepreneuring my way to fame and fortune with a bankroll of petro-bucks after I had charmed a couple of shieks and shiekettes. I was traveling through the Mid-East at the time and had made friends with some well-placed Arabs of the rich variety who had been kind enough to show me the sights of Damascus and take me to dinner. I had invested in a Berlitz Arabic dictionary and was proud of the progress I thought I had made in learning that elusive language. Upon the conclusion of dinner with my rich Arabs friends, a dinner that I had reason to believe would lead me to great fortune, I stood up and shook hands with each of my dinner partners, solemnly intoning "Ahnee-bahib" while smiling my friendliest smile. I thought I was saying "I like you" and was therefore somewhat taken aback when their expressions reflected unrestrained horror and they quickly excused themselves never to be seen by me again. A quick reference to the Berlitz showed me that I had slightly mispronounced the well-meant phrase and was instead saying "You are an animal". The only good that came out of the unfortunate incident was that I was suddenly fluent with an Arab vulgarism that proved handy when insults were necessary.

Now I stick to English, entertaining the notion that I'm a writer. "Money" tells me that this monolingualism will insure my financial downfall. I, however, would just as soon die poor than be attacked for asking the time of day.

The Gold-Plated Mouth

My wife says this is the tackiest thing I've ever done. But I think she's just jealous.

I've never been big on jewelry. Glitter just hasn't been my game.

I don't own a watch, much less a gold Rolex that could cost as much as my car.

The only ring I have or want is the one my wife gave me on the day we were married. No diamond pinkies for me.

I stopped wearing chains around my neck when someone stole the St. Christopher's medal out of my gym locker back in high school.

And the only time I ever wore an earring was once on Halloween. I greatly regretted it.

So you can understand my reluctance when my dentist suggested a gold tooth.

"A gold tooth?" I exclaimed. "Isn't that a bit excessive?"

"It might cost a little more, but it will last forever," my dentist said.

"Can't you show me something nice in, uh, plastic?" I asked.

"It will taste like you've just eaten a model airplane," he said.

"What about wood? George Washington had wood teeth you know."

"You'll die of terminal splinters."

"There are no alternatives?"

"Well, there is porcelain."

I thought about porcelain. The only thing I know about porcelain is that it is used to make commodes.

"Go with the gold," I told my dentist.

"You'll love it. It will look great," he said.

I had my doubts. When I think of gold teeth, I think of Ali the Turk.

Ali the Turk ran the pawn shop in my hometown. I think he bought his mouth at Tiffany's.

Not only did he have gold teeth, but he had designs cut into the gold— crescent moons, stars, even a big "A" for Ali right up front.

On slow days, some of us used to drop by the pawn shop just to look at Ali's teeth. It beat watching them put up the "special" signs at the A&P.

Every one of Ali's gold teeth had a story.

"This one," said Ali, pointing to a bicuspid, "is from Atlee Spoondecker's high school class ring. And this one — " a particularly ostentatious molar— "is what's left of that tacky brooch that Gladys Gillright's grandmother left her."

Ali the Turk said he wore gold in his mouth because in his native land it was a sign of great wealth.

I guess he was rich. All I know is that when Ali the Turk died, undertakers from 14 nearby states bid for the job. The guy who finally won used Ali's teeth to finance a chain of cut-rate crematoriums. But that's another story.

I should tell you how I came to require a gold tooth.

It all started a couple of months ago when I went out for a pizza with some friends. I chomped down on my pizza. It was an anchovy pizza. I have reason to believe the anchovies were petrified.

At any rate, the tooth broke. It was a big old molar that had served me well for years and suddenly it was cracked in two.

When I visited the dentist, I asked him if he thought I could sue the pizza joint that served me petrified anchovies.

"No way," he said. "You've got such lousy teeth they could break chewing ice water."

The reason I have lousy teeth is because I do not floss. I used to floss, but the reason I don't floss anymore is because the last time I did it I managed to get the floss stuck and when I yanked it out I chipped off another tooth.

So much for my dental hygiene. I figure if God really wanted us not to have food between our teeth, he wouldn't have created barbecue ribs.

But with my brand new gold tooth, I don't have to worry about tooth decay. Gold, my friends, does not rot.

From the moment my gold tooth was installed I fell in love with it. I can chomp down on just about anything now. I'm even thinking of getting my file out and sharpening that sucker up so I can save money by buying cheaper cuts of meat.

But the best thing is that it just looks so very flashy. I spend a lot of time grinning these days, with hopes that someone will comment on my oral splendor. I give them a couple of seconds and if they don't compliment me on my gold tooth then I just say something subtle like: "Hey! You wanna take a look inside my mouth?"

Everyone is impressed. So much so that I've even been thinking about getting my whole mouth done up in gold, with crescent moons and stars, the whole works.

I'll be opening the pawn shop next week. Give you $25 for that old high school ring.

A Basic Fix-it Guide

My basic rule for home repairs is this: If you can't make something work by beating it with a hammer, then it's time to call for help.

One of the secrets to a happy home life is knowing how to fix things.

Used to be that people were pretty handy when it came to repairs. Everyone had tools and knew what to do with them.

Nowadays this doesn't hold true. Most people either don't know how to fix things or would rather get someone to fix things for them. This causes problems all around and is the primary reason for the ever-increasing divorce rate and the declining quality of life.

That's why it's important for you to become a handyman. Or handywoman as the case may be, although identifying yourself by this latter title will only open the way for unwelcome remarks.

First thing you need is tools. Take all your spare cash — this should come to something like $23 — put it in your pocket and go to the K-Mart or some other place that sells things cheap. Don't carry credit cards or a checkbook because these cheapo places try to sucker you in by running lots of "Amazing Special Values" and you will be tempted to buy something like a three-speed electric drill with reverse function for a low $89.95 when a tool like that can only get you into trouble.

A good rule to follow is this: "Don't buy any tool that needs to be plugged in." Tools that need to be plugged in invariably carry messages that say: "WARNING — Use only on 110 volt systems with 15 amp resistance and 100 ohm rating." This is electricity talk and what it really means is that if you don't look out you can get killed.

So concentrate on the basic stuff. Here is a simple checklist:

1. Hammer — Ask the salesman for a left-handed model. He will laugh at this little witticism and because he has heard it a million times and is sick and tired of it, he will then leave you to do your shopping in peace.

2. Screwdrivers — They make two different kinds, but no one can ever remember their names except retired mid-level management types with too much time on their hands. Anyway, get one of each and make up your own names for them. It's easier that way. I call mine Sado and Masochism.

3. Nuts and bolts — I never have figured out which is which but since they usually get used together it really doesn't make any difference. Get at least five pounds of mixed nuts and bolts because they are always falling behind your washing machine where you can't get them out.

4. Wrench — You use this when working with nuts and bolts. Whatever you do don't buy one of those sets that has a whole bunch of wrenches marked ⅝ and ⅛ and ¾. You'll spend all your time trying to pick out the right one and, as luck would have it, you're probably trying to fix something with metric parts and nothing will work. Better to get an adjustable wrench that will get rusty and freeze up on you. Make sure it's big and heavy so you can just whop the dickens out of whatever you're trying to fix.

5. Duck tape — Spend a lot of money on this. It's good stuff. Taxidermists use it to reassemble water fowl that have been blown to smithereens by hunters. Hence, its name. It is also used in air conditioning ducks.

When you get home with all your tools get right to work while the momentum is with you. Take advantage of this because it won't last long. Make a loud announcement, stating your plans. Say something like: "Well, I'm going to get to work fixing that broken framus."

Get out all your tools and make a lot of noise. Every now and then, yell for your spouse to bring you more beer. They usually comply readily to this request because you are being such a trooper by trying to fix something.

After about an hour — or a six-pack, whichever comes first — go next door and ask your neighbor for help. Most neighbors respond quite willingly to calls for help and, if you're lucky, generally know how to fix things.

If this doesn't work, call your realtor and put your house up for sale. When looking for a new place to live, study the garages of your prospective neighbors. Try to move next door to someone who has a disgustingly neat garage with hooks on the wall to hold all kinds of tools and little jars filled with nuts and bolts and screws and gizmos that you are all the time needing but never seem to have.

On your first day in the new house, introduce yourself to the neighbor and say: "Hey, I just want you to know that if there's anything I can ever do to help you out just let me know. And if there's anything I've got that you want to borrow, then just feel free to ask."

The next day, walk over and ask if he'll fix that broken framus for you. After that, everything should fall into place.

How To Run A Newspaper

After reading this you'll understand why I'll never get to be an executive editor.

These are depressing times if you happen to be in the newspaper business. Just look at what has happened in the past few months.

The Washington Star has gone out of business. The Philadelphia Bulletin may soon go out of business. Even the New York Daily News, with millions of readers, is on shaky ground.

It's not much fun running a newspaper. I can say this from experience. I used to run a newspaper. It was a weekly down in Marathon called the Florida Keys Free Press.

The guy who owned the Free Press had made lots of money in the shrimp business. He thought it would be kind of neat to have his own newspaper, so he started one up and hired some people who didn't know beans about the business. When it became evident that they couldn't even tell the difference between a paragraph and a Pontiac, much less write worth a darn, he fired them all and hired five of us fresh out of college to take over.

I thought it would be a great journalistic experience. I had visions of spending my time writing hard-hitting editorials and incisive investigative reports and, in general, raking a lot of muck in the Keys. What really happened was that the Free Press was losing $5,000 a week and I spent all my time trying to sell advertising and collecting on past due accounts and convincing our creditors to let us postpone payments until things got better. I even delivered the paper door to door every Thursday morning.

As it turned out, one of the owner's big, expensive shrimp boats caught on fire and sank. The next day, I walked into the office and all the phones had been pulled out of the walls and the typesetting equipment was gone. The Free Press had folded. The owner figured that buying a new shrimp boat was more important than losing $5,000 a week on a newspaper. He was probably right.

As rotten as my brief tenure of running a newspaper was, I still get the longing every now and then to do it again. I like to sit around and dream about how I would run my newspaper. Here's what I'd do:

- I'd give less space to the President of the United States and all his lackeys. Of course, if he did anything really big and important I'd run a story about it. But this rarely happens. Mostly presidents just talk about what they'd like to do. Most people I know would rather read stories about crime and scandal and disaster than be bored by the pipedreams of presidents.
- I'd apply the above policy to local politicians and government bodies. If they do something for the voters, then I'd run a story. If they're just running off their mouths and engaging in polical chicanery then let them buy advertising if they want the public to know about it.
- I'd have something funny on the front page every day. After reading all about crime and scandal and disaster, people deserve a little laugh.
- I'd hire a bunch of young kids to go out on the street and yell "EXTRA! EXTRA! READ ALL ABOUT IT!" and sell my newspa-

per. Most newspapers don't do this anymore. But it would be great for business. I don't know anyone who can turn down young kids selling anything.

• I'd make my sportswriters report on other subjects from time to time. Like city council meetings or concerts by the symphony orchestra. Sportswriters are generally very insightful craftsmen and pick up on things that other reporters might miss. A New York newspaper used to do this with its sportswriters years ago. It once sent a sportswriter out to review a concert featuring Leopold Stakowski, the famous conductor. The story began: "Leopold Stakowski played Brahms Friday night. Brahms lost." We need more stories like that.

• I'd make my other reporters go out and cover sports every now and then. As good as they are, sportswriters miss some things every now and then. I'd make my reporters write about whether the seats at a ballpark are comfortable and if the concession stand is any good.

• I'd sit down once a year and write a story about all the mistakes my newspaper had made during the previous 365 days. It would be good reading.

• I'd run more stories about giant zucchini and pigs that are born with five legs and ducks that play with dogs and other stuff that falls into the category of "backyard phenomena." Most newspapers stopped running these kind of stories a long time ago. Everyone I know misses them.

• I'd keep a close watch on my photographers and not let them sneak any pictures of sunsets or pelicans sitting on old docks or boats sillhouted against the sky into the paper. All these pictures look alike and are a waste of space. I'd make them take more pictures of pretty girls in bathing suits.

• And finally, I'd keep a close watch on my columnists. I'd pay them handsomely, but make sure they didn't have any extra time to sit around and dream up ways to change my newspaper. It only causes trouble.

Your Basic Bar

The best thing about writing this column was that I got umpteen invitations from good bars for me to come around and have a beer to see if they met my qualifications. That's why I plan on writing more columns like this in the future.

I met a friend for a drink the other day. He was buying, so he got to pick the bar.

It was one of those fancy, new bars.

I will be straight out about it: I do not like those fancy, new bars.

Fancy, new bars have too many gimmicks. They pay too much attention to creating a certain "atmosphere." They ignore the main reason people go to bars and that, quite simply, is to just sit and drink and think about things for awhile without all the atmosphere getting in the way.

This fancy, new bar I went to had a cutesy name. I'm not looking to cause trouble, so I won't identify the place. But you are probably familiar with the cutesy names bars use these days. And they've got cutesy themes to go along with the cutesy names.

This place looked as if it was trying to be a bar like Rick's Place in "Casablanca." There were highbacked wicker chairs and tiffany lamps and potted palms all over the place and the waitresses ran around in khaki shirts and khaki shorts like they were getting ready to go on safari.

I ordered a beer. It cost $1.75.

That's the main thing I've got against these fancy, new bars. They charge too much for all the atmosphere. For what you spend on a few beers you can put a down payment on an airplane ticket to the real Casablanca.

Besides that, I can never tell where the men's room is in these places. They've even got cutesy names on the bathroom doors, names like "Buoys," or "Dudes" or "Bwana." I will sneak over to a potted palm before I walk through a door that says "Bwana."

Since I'm on the subject, and since this column only deals with topics of the utmost social significance, let me tell you what makes a good bar.

The name doesn't make much difference. It can just be called "Joe's" or "Fred's" or something. The only sort of cutesy name I go for is "Dew Drop Inn." I've never gone into a "Dew Drop Inn" that I didn't like. I can even remember coming out of a few of them.

Great attention should be paid to beer. It's OK to have liquor, but beer should be the main attraction. For the $1.75 that you put down at a fancy, new bar you should be able to buy three drafts at a good bar. And you ought to be able to buy a decent-sized pitcher for what you pay for a six-pack at the grocery store.

Here are some other items that need attending to:

Juke Boxes: No bar is worth a darn without a decent juke box. And it should have plenty of old songs on it, plenty of songs that you can sing along with after you've had a pitcher of beer. It helps if they are sorrowful songs, songs about lovin' and losin' and how somebody done somebody wrong.

Food: Peanuts, hot sausages and pickled eggs. None of this junk that they put out during so-called "Happy Hours" at the fancy, new bars. A good bar doesn't need "Happy Hour."

I have a friend named Rosco who runs a good bar. Someone told Rosco he needed to have a "Happy Hour" and put out a table of food to keep up with the competition.

"Why, hell yes, I'd be glad to," Rosco said.

Next day, Rosco walked into his bar carrying some boxes and laid them on a table.

"Y'all c'mon and eat up," he shouted.

Then he opened up the boxes to reveal a few dozen fresh tomatoes straight from Immokalee. That's as fancy as it needs to get.

The Hired Help: Personally, I prefer big, homely women with hearts of gold behind the bar. If they're too pretty it takes your attention off the beer and the juke boxes and you could wind up in trouble. These big, homely women should also know more jokes than you do, but still be willing to laugh at the ones you tell them.

Diversions: Like I've said before, just sitting and drinking and listening to the juke box should come first, but if there must be something else then it should be a pool table. But that's it. Under no conditions should there be any of those computer games that make noises that clash with the music.

Regular customers:A good bar should always have at least one sloppy, old drunk who drapes himself over a stool and makes a fool out of himself. This is to remind you what might happen if you don't call it a night and go home.

That about does it.

And just writing all this has given me quite a thirst. Think it's time to step out and find a good bar. I've got exactly $2 in my pocket. Those big, homely women don't mind if you don't alway leave 'em a tip.

A Tour of Kennesaw

No, I don't own a gun.

Good morning, y'all, and welcome to Kennesaw, Georgia, the community we're proud to call "The Shootingest Li'l Town in America."

We're glad you've joined us to help celebrate the 25th Anniversary of Kennesaw's famous gun ordinance.

Yes, it was way back in 1982 that the town fathers, sensing a decay in the moral fiber throughout our country, got together and passed their farsighted law requiring all citizens to own at least one gun.

We've come a long way since then in our quest to preserve law and order and promote our basic, savage instincts. Today, Kennesaw is a spirited community where the motto: "All for guns and guns for all," truly prevails.

Before stepping on the tour bus and entering the city limits, we kindly ask that you stop by the quaint "Ye Olde Weapon Bin," just past past the ticket booth, and strap on the gun of your choice.

You menfolk will appreciate the fine selection of automatic weaponry available, including that time-honored classic— the Thompson submachine gun— and the ever-popular AK-47, with its kill-potential of 26.4 per second, enough to wipe out the whole busload of you quicker than you can say "God Bless the Second Amendment." Heh-heh.

For you little ladies, a variety of sleek handguns can be found. The .357 Magnum will fit nicely into most purses. But for real firepower we suggest the double-action .44 Magnum revolver. Just imagine— 240 grains of hot lead exploding out of a big barrel in your hand at 1200 feet per second, and super accurate even on a running target.

And for the small fry, there are plenty of BB and pellet guns just waiting for their eager, little hands— the perfect starting point for their future weapon efficiency.

Vendors will be stationed throughout the bus and live ammunition can be purchased for as little as $2.50 a round for those of you who'd enjoy some recreational sniping during the tour.

Now, if you'll take your seats. . . POW! POW!. . . Down, you in the back! . . . we'll proceed down Bull's-Eye Boulevard, Kennesaw's main drag.

On your left is "Shady Oaks," Kennesaw's first cemetery. We now boast 17 burial grounds and construction has just begun on a beautiful 32-story mausoleum, since vacant land is becoming so hard to find.

"Shady Oaks" was filled to capacity within two years after the gun ordinance was passed and is the final resting place for every single one of the city fathers who voted in favor of the ordinance.

"Live by the gun, die by the gun," as we say here in Kennesaw. Heh-heh.

If, after the tour is over, you'd like to pay your respects to these brave men, then it is customary to stand in front of their graves and fire a few rounds in the air in salute of their achievements.

The townsfolk you see lined up there on the sidewalk are all waiting to get in "Shoot 'Em Up Sally's," the newest of Kennesaw's 27 public shooting ranges. "Shoot 'Em Up Sally's" is open 24 hours a day and features moving targets that resemble various ethnic minorities, all of which drip real blood when you score a lethal hit.

If your finger cramps up at the shooting range, then you can always step next door to the Kennesaw Moving Picture House which only shows movies starring Charles Bronson and Clint Eastwood before he put down his guns and started fooling around with that silly chimpanzee.

Look out! Everyone hit the deck!

Whoo, that was a close one. Seems as if we got caught in yet another little skirmish between the Widow Barker and the Widow Brown. Not a day goes by that they don't get in an argument over who bakes the best peach cobbler. And, as you well know, in Kennesaw there's only one way to settle those little spats. I guess it's a good thing those ol' gals are nearly blind, although their poor aim does waste some innocent tourists every now and then.

Our tour will wind up here at the former site of the Kennesaw courthouse, now the location of the newest Kennesaw Gunshot Clinic, one of 12 such facilities in town.

You're welcome to step out now and do some sightseeing in

Kennesaw. We think you'll find us a friendly, little town, providing, of course, you don't try to push any of your fancy-schmancy, out-of-town ways over on us.

If you're looking for a place to spend the night, I'd recommend the Kennesaw Inn, the only problem being that all the rooms are currently filled up. But if you'd like to take matters into your own hands, then just feel free to fire away and create a few vacancies.

So, like I said, get off the bus.

I'll give you to the count of three.

The Mark Of An Old Man

My back still gives me a little trouble now and then. Usually when it's time to wash the car.

I stopped being a young man at approximately 10 a.m. last Friday.

It doesn't matter that I am only 31, soon to be 32. Throw chronology out the window. Years don't mean a thing.

Not when you've got a bad back. When you've got a bad back you feel like an old man. It's as simple as that.

I suppose I would still be young if I'd just broken down and bought one of those electric garage door openers.

But no. I don't go for gadgets.

"Just one more fancy-schmancy gizmo that will cost a lot of money and then go on the blink," I told my wife when she suggested that an electric garage door opener was just the thing we needed. "People get too pampered by machines these days. There's absolutely no reason why we can't open the garage door with our own two hands. Good exercise."

Everything went just fine until last Friday. That's when I bent down, grabbed the garage door handle and yanked up, not knowing the blasted thing was locked.

In cases like this, something, as they say, has to give.

I gave.

To be more precise, that part of my body known as the lumbar region — the lower back to those of you who are anatomically ignorant— did the old Rice Krispies routine. Snap, crackle, pop and I was flattened.

If you've never had occasion to lay face down on the floor of your garage, let me recommend that you plan ahead, making sure you have cleaned up the oil drippings leaked by your car. Most people I know don't look good smeared with 30-weight. Besides, when one is already humbled by pain, further indiginities, even those of a cosmetic nature, are totally devastating.

I finally made it up on the third try. Not all the way up, mind you, but at least I was ambulatory. You might say I was a walking right angle.

At this point, I should mention that I am one of those people who, when things of a physical nature go wrong, expects sympathy. I like to be pampered when I'm hurting. Nothing extravagant. Being waited on hand and foot is sufficient.

I hobbled into the house.

"Who are you?" my wife asked. "The Hunchback of Notre Dame?"

Funny lady.

"Honey, I threw my back out," I managed to moan. "It's killing me."

This is your basic cue for sympathy. You know, help me to the couch, slip off my shoes and bring me something cool to drink. Say soothing things like: "There, there. It will be OK," or "You poor, poor thing."

What I got was laughter. Lots of laughter. Unending laughter.

And then the kicker: "If you think this means you're going to get out of washing the car, you're crazy."

I thought a good night's sleep would cure my ailment. But there was a major flaw to that theory. Namely, I couldn't sleep. I would toss one way, my back would turn the other and the result was sheer agony.

And when I got out of bed the next morning— slid out is more like it— I was stiffer than I was the night before. I groaned on my journey to the bathroom. My wife laughed at that, too.

Since then I've been adjusting to life with a bad back. Like I said before, there is nothing else — midriff bulge, wrinkles, even gray hair— that can make you feel more like an old man.

Tying my shoes is a major undertaking. Getting out of the car requires delicate manuevering. Forget about going up steps.

A friend recommended some exercises that might help. I got down on the floor to do them. I couldn't get up.

Another friend recommended a chiropractor. But that's not for me, buddy. I watch "60 Minutes." I saw what that chiropractor did to Mike Wallace. I heard the bones crack. Uh-uh. No way.

The only good to come of my busted back is that now I have a truly legitimate excuse for not going jogging.

Which means I'll just sit around, get fat and grow old.

I have plenty of time to look at the newspaper now. I've been checking the ads for electric garage door openers. I'm going to have one installed for my wife.

Then I'm going to hide out with the remote control in my hand and just when she pulls under the door — zap!— I'm going to lower the boom.

Just thinking about it makes me laugh.

Oh, it hurts.

A Representative Of The People

Thank God for politicians. Otherwise, newspaper columnists would really have to scramble to find something to write about.

I called up Congressman Handintill to find out about all this sex and drug business on Capitol Hill.

"The Congressman is tied up in a meeting," his aide told me. "May I ask the nature of your call?"

"I need to find out where I'm supposed to drop off the briefcase with the $25,000 in it," I said.

Two seconds later Handintill was on the line.

"Ha, ha. Funny joke," he said. "You're with the F.B.I., right?"

"No way."

"Prove it."

"J. Edgar Hoover wore lace panties," I said.

"He did not. They were silk. . . uh, never mind. I believe you," he said. "And by the way, you might fool a Richard Kelley with that $25,000 bit, but I'm above that. Way above that. I charge $100,000 just to introduce a special interest bill, much less seeing that it gets passed."

"I'll keep that in mind, sir," I said.

"I suppose you're calling about this so-called scandal involving the Congressional pages?"

"You got it. What's the story?"

"There's no scandal. It's all blown out of proportion."

"You mean Congressmen aren't really having homosexual relations with minors? You mean Congressmen aren't really trading certain privileges for sexual favors? You mean Congressmen aren't really trafficking in drugs?"

"Now, wait a minute. I didn't say that."

"Then it's all true?"

"Of course it's all true. But there's no scandal. There's nothing wrong with it."

"Congressman Handintill! How can you say that? As representatives of the American people. . ."

"Stop right there. You've hit the nail on the head."

"I have?"

"Certainly. Congress is merely representative of the American people. It is our duty to mirror society."

"I'm afraid I don't understand."

"Well, just like your typical American community, Congress is made up of people from all walks of life. There are bankers. There are businessmen. There are housewives. There are. . ."

"There are too damn many lawyers. Congress has an overabundance of lawyers."

"What did I tell you? Just like your typical American community."

"Hmmm. I see your point. I guess that's why there are no honest auto mechanics in Congress."

"Not to mention the absence of clean-living journalists."

"Indeed. But how do you justify sex and drugs?"

"Quite simply. What percentage of the American public uses drugs or engages in illicit sex?"

"Oh, I guess about 20 percent and that's probably a conservative estimate."

"You're probably right. Now there are 535 members of Congress and no more than six of them are thought to be involved with illicit sex and drugs. May I point out that that is only 1.1 percent of our membership?"

"Gee, maybe this whole thing has been blown out of proportion. Compared to the rest of the country, Congress comes off cleaner than choirboys."

"Exactly. That's the problem."

"It is?"

"Why certainly. Congress is far too virtuous, disgustingly so. How can we be expected to fairly represent the American people if we don't share their vices as well as their virtues? And I'll be the first to admit that we are shockingly remiss in the vice department."

"You are?"

"Oh my, yes. We're way behind the percentages in gambling, mugging and murdering, although we definitely hold our own in prostitution and grand larceny. And when it comes to drugs and illicit sex, well, I'm doing my best to see that we make some progress in that area, too."

"How?"

"As chairman of the House Immoral Activities Committee, a sort of Affirmative Action plan for degenerates, I am recruiting my fellow Congressmen to take a more active role in illicit sex and drug use so that we can be even more representative of our constituents. I'm proud to say that all 535 members of Congress have volunteered their services."

"Well, Congressman Handintill, I commend you on your concern. And keep up the good work."

"I intend to. And, as a special favor to you, I'll gladly reduce my rates and allow you to bribe me for a mere $25,000."

"Great. How should I arrange to get the money to you?"

"Don't worry. I'll send a young boy over to pick it up."

One Of Those Days

The day after this column appeared, I received 17 chain letters. I'm no fool. I answered every single one.

It was one of those days.

I went out to get the paper and it wasn't there. My neighbors all had their papers in the driveways. But mine wasn't there.

I stood on the front lawn, shocked that the newspaper carrier would actually make good on his threat to cut off my subscription if I didn't pay up.

Then I turned around and headed back inside. I picked up four sandspurs in my right foot and two in my left. The boy who mows our lawn has been promising for a week that he would get by and do his job.

I pulled the sandspurs from my feet and got splinters in my fingers. I flicked the sandspurs on the grass and noticed that it wasn't really grass, but weeds that looked like grass. I am paying a boy who never shows up $8.50 a week to take care of my weeds. Besides that, he never sharpens his blades.

I walked into the kitchen and filled the coffee pot with water. Then I opened the coffee can. It was empty.

I heated some water for tea. I hate tea. I put the tea bag in the cup and poured the hot water over it. I jiggled the tea bag around and the string broke. When I fished out the tea bag I burned my fingers and knocked the cup on the floor.

The cup didn't break because it landed on one of the cats. The cat started howling. That woke up my son.

My son was standing up in his bed crying. He had managed to squirm out of his diapers and the stuff that was inside was smeared everywhere. I kissed him on the cheek. The stuff was there, too.

I cleaned him up, got his bottle and put him in bed with his mother. Before long, they were both asleep again.

I was wide awake, there was no newspaper and I was out of coffee. I flipped on the "Today" show. Jane was on vacation and that wimpy guy was substituting for Willard. I flipped it off.

I decided to run a couple of miles. Just when I'd hit my pace, two lean guys raced up from behind and passed me. I loped by the bus stop and a couple of third-graders started snickering.

"He looks funny," one of them said.

When I got home I opened the door and the cats ran out. They'll get fleas. Then they'll get tapeworms. Then the vet will charge me $30 to clean them out.

I watered the beautiful Rapus palm in the corner of our living room. It cost $300. It has terminal mealy bugs and should be dead in a month or two. Then I can watch the Ficus tree on the other side of the room lose its leaves and die, too.

I got in the shower. The water never warmed up because I'd forgotten to plug in the water heater. We're trying to save on the electric bill. Drying off, I looked out the window and saw that the outside lights had been left on all night. The porch fan had been left running, too.

I went to turn off the lights and the fan. I noticed that the stereo turntable was spinning round and round. I hadn't listened to an album in a couple of days. Funny.

I decided to get dressed and go to work. I tried to pull a pair of pants out of the closet, but the clothes hanger was caught on another clothes hanger. I pulled harder and the clothes rack unsnapped and all my clothes wound up on the closet floor.

I cussed. That woke up my son and my wife. One started crying and the other started complaining.

I got dressed and drove into the office. I got out of the car and noticed a funny smell. I opened the hood and saw smoke coming from the place where I was supposed to have put in some oil a couple of weeks ago. I closed the hood without investigating further.

I went through the mail on my desk. I found an invitation to a cocktail party that I really wanted to attend. It took place last Saturday.

I sat down at my typewriter and tried to think of something to write about. It's been three hours and the sheet is still blank.

I got a chain letter in the mail a couple of weeks ago. The chain letter warned that if I didn't make copies and pass them on to five friends then something terrible would happen to me in the month of December. I threw the chain letter in the garbage can.

It's not even November yet. I don't think I'll survive.

I hope whoever sent me that chain letter is reading this column. Send me another one. Please. Give me another chance.

Take This Advice And. . .

Most people love to give advice. It compensates for their inability to set good examples.

I don't mind people giving me advice from time to time. In fact, there are occasions when I welcome their kind counsel.

For instance, a hurricane comes along and blows the roof off my house. An acquaintance drops by and says: "Here's $10,000. I suggest you take it, buy a new roof and don't worry about paying me back."

That's the kind of advice I like. Trouble is, that's not the kind of advice I get.

The advice I get is usually unsolicited and always unwelcome. It comes from people who would do society a favor by minding their own business.

For instance, a hurricane comes along and blows the roof off my house. I am blessed with an acquaintance who drops by and says: "That should teach you not to use cheap tarpaper shingles. I suggest you use a high-quality tile from now on."

We all encounter people like this. And we all encounter problems dealing with them.

It would be a simple matter to say: "Shut up. Go away. Mind your own business."

But that's not civilized. That's not polite. And while the people who offer unsolicited advice are indeed jerks, they are generally well-meaning jerks and deserve to be treated as such.

Which means we must not be blatantly rude. A subtle rudeness is much more fitting.

Now, there are a few major categories in which these well-meaning jerks offer their advice. Let's study them to see how best to make the proper responses.

The care and nutrition of a newborn child is a natural arena for unsolicited advice. Well-meaning jerks seem to know everything about taking care of your baby.

Say you are in a department store and your baby starts to cry, as babies so often do. Invariably, a well-meaning jerk, usually a total stranger, will walk up and say: "I think it must be hungry."

Do not give in to the impulse to throttle the busybody. Simply look him or her straight in the eye and in your most pleasant voice reply: "My child could not possibly be hungry. I fed the little thing the day before yesterday."

A similar strategy can be used upon neighbors who choose to offer comment on the sad shape of your lawn, another category in which too much advice is too freely dispensed.

You've no doubt had a neighbor approach you and say: "Your lawn is a disgrace to the neighborhood. I suggest you mow it and then spread a good organic fertilizer over it."

Do not cower in the face of this assault. Immediately respond: "Fear not, my good man. The goats are on their way. I've ordered six for the front and six for the back and they'll take care of all my mowing and fertilizing chores for me. And, because you're such a nice guy, I'll be glad to let them wander over to graze at your place every now and then."

But the most common subject that well-meaning jerks are likely to advise us on is one in which we all hold our own sacred notions — the art of backyard barbecuing.

If you are ever planning a long, adventurous journey through uncharted terrain, then it's a good idea to take along charcoal, lighter fluid, matches and a grill. If you become hopelessly lost and in need of help, simply strike up the fire. Someone is bound to jump out of the bushes and give you more help and advice than you'd ever believe.

Such was recently my experience when I made the mistake of inviting a well-meaning jerk over to eat some steaks.

First he instructed me in the proper way to stack the charcoal.

Next he educated me as to exactly how long the lighter fluid should soak in. Then he suggested ways in which I could maximize the ventilation. Finally he enlightened me as to the best procedure for testing the doneness of the meat.

At that point I sent him inside to help my wife make cocktails.

When we sat down to eat, all he could do was complain.

Gee, could I help it that his was the only steak burnt to a crisp?

Waiting For The Bale

This one goes out for the square grouper fishermen of Florida, true sportsmen one and all. It's also in honor of Warlock, who told me the story and promptly lost his job after I wrote about it in the paper. He wound up joining the Navy, but still dreams of the day when his ship will come in.

They had stopped on the sixth floor for the morning ritual. There were five of them, a crew of electricians, and they were scheduled to work on the 11th floor that day, installing conduit on the penthouse deck of the fancy condominium.

But it wasn't a good idea for the morning ritual to take place on the top floor. People might see what was going on. So they had found a private place on the sixth floor with a nice view of the Gulf.

Like any other job, construction work on high-rises has its pros and cons. There's an element of danger, a chance of taking the Big Step. Fall off anywhere above two stories and there's the very real possibility you will be a dead man shortly after landing. A definite con.

But the view makes up for it. The view from the sixth floor of a Gulf-front highrise, early in the morning when the water is still and the birds are diving for fish, is nothing short of stupendous.

Let's just say the morning ritual enhanced the view. The

morning ritual consisted of smoking a few joints and drinking some coffee. Then the five of them would sit around and shoot the bull a little while before going to work.

Wild Man, the piping foreman, the one with the full beard, the gold earring and the big motorcycle, was the first to see it. It was floating a couple of hundred yards offshore.

"It's a bale!" he shouted. "It's a goddam bale of pot!"

If there was one thing they had spent plenty of time shooting the bull about, fantasizing actually, it was that some day they might luck onto a bale of pot that had washed ashore. With all the boats running dope in the Gulf, tons and tons of Columbia's finest, it wasn't unlikely that one might float their way.

Local legends had grown out of such experiences. There were those guys on Sanibel — construction workers, just like them — who had hauled in nearly 400 pounds of the stuff one morning. And just the week before, nine bales had washed up at the county park a few miles south of their job site.

Yes, it seemed, after all this waiting, their bale had come in.

"Damn, that's what it is all right — a square grouper. Yeeehawwwww!" yelled Warlock, the one with the shaved head and beads. At 18, he was the youngest of them.

"Sure is," said Barnacle, the ex-marine. "I can see the plastic wrapper and the burlap around it."

"Boys," said Chief Two Fingers, the foreman, who was nicknamed after his love of tequila, "we're gonna be in the money."

Figure a bale of pot weighs in at 100 pounds. Use a conservative estimate of selling it for $200 a pound, after you've cut out a little stash for personal use, of course, and you are talking roughly $20,000. Split it five ways and you've got $4,000 apiece. Quite a nice little tax-free gift from the sea.

They watched it float for 15 minutes or so, figuring out how they would get it to shore and, even better, how they each would spend their share of the profit.

"I've got some car repairs that are long overdue," said Trigger Lip, the one who always seemed to be griping about something.

"I plan to do some serious partying," said Barnacle.

"Me, too," said Wild Man. "Take a long vacation and treat myself right."

"I'll do some serious partying and then if there's anything left, maybe a little sensible spending," said Chief Two Fingers. "But first we gotta get the damn thing in here. Warlock, you run down to the marina and see if we can't borrow a boat. Tell 'em it's an emergency. Hell, pay 'em for it if you have to, but, for God's sake, don't tell 'em what it's for."

Warlock was running down the six flights of stairs before all the words were out of Chief Two Fingers' mouth. And all the way he was thinking about his cut and how he was going to spend it. First, he'd pay off his car and then maybe he'd have a little left over for the down payment on some land. This was the chance he'd been waiting for, that they'd all been waiting for; a chance to get ahead.

Warlock was running for the marina when he heard Chief Two Fingers yell: "C'mon back. Forget it."

Warlock stopped and looked up to the sixth floor.

"Something wrong?" he asked.

"Yeah," said Wild Man, "our bale just up and flew away. It was a damn old pelican. I swear, I haven't ever seen a pelican sit still that long."

"Time to get to work," said Chief Two Fingers.

The next day, during the morning ritual, none of them said anything about the dark, squarish thing floating a couple of hundred yards off shore. But they kept watching it. And, sure enough, it up and flew away after a few minutes, too.

The Girl Scout Cookie Scam

I received about a dozen phone calls about this column from Girl Scout leaders who thought it was just terrible. I suggested that they should start working on their sense of humor merit badge.

The doorbell rang and through the little peephole I could see the two Girl Scouts waiting for me to open up.

I knew their scam. They wanted to sell me cookies.

I don't like Girl Scout cookies. I don't even like Girl Scouts.

Call me a jerk, but I've got my reasons. It all goes back to when I was a Boy Scout.

One weekend our Boy Scout troop went camping. Our scoutmaster was a guy by the name of Jinks Wordley. Mr. Wordley's idea of supervision was to settle into his Winnebago with a jug of Jim Beam and a deck of playing cards, then commence a marathon game of poker with some buddies while we Boy Scouts ran wild through the woods. It was just great by us.

While running wild through the woods on this particular trip, we discovered a Girl Scout troop camped nearby. We were having a good time yelling at them when their troop leader approached us with a proposition.

"Would you boys be interested in a test of your skills as outdoorsmen?" she asked.

You name it, we told her. After all, we were Boy Scouts.

The Girl Scout leader laid down the rules — Boy Scouts against Girl Scouts with each group given half a day to go out in the woods and forage for supper. The winner would be the group that made the best meal. The losers would have to wash dishes and clean up after the winners for the rest of the weekend.

We Boy Scouts snickered and headed off into the woods. A couple of us made fishing poles and attacked a nearby pond. Others got busy building intricate snares and traps, the better to catch squirrels and rabbits with. A few whittled out bows and arrows and announced they were going after dove and quail.

But when our time was up the only one who'd gotten anything was Pee Wee Braun. Pee Wee had butchered a bunch of toads and was trying to pass off the results as frog legs. No one was exactly digging in.

The Girl Scouts, on the other hand, had assembled quite a spread. They had at least a dozen different dishes cooking on the fire — tiny green cattails that tasted like corn on the cob and potfuls of swamp cabbage. They had a big bowl of salad made out of dandelions and chicory and other such roughage.

"Shoot, that ain't food," complained Pee Wee Braun. "Where's the meat?"

"Shut up and start washing the dishes," said Mr. Wordley.

It turned out to be a terrible weekend and I've been convinced ever since that it's harmful to learn humility at such an early age.

The other reason I don't like Girl Scouts is because they invented "S'mores." S'mores are made by placing hot roasted marshmallows on a Hershey bar and then sticking that gooey mess between a couple of graham crackers. Girl Scouts are addicted to S'mores. Even former Girl Scouts who are now grown women cannot kick the S'more habit.

Women like my wife, for instance. On our absolutely last camping trip together, my wife insisted on bringing along the ingredients for S'mores. I objected, saying we should only take canned goods — Vienna sausage, Beenie Weenies, sardines and sensible stuff like that.

The ants attacked about two in the morning. And since the marshmallows, chocolate and graham crackers were in the pack I was using for a pillow, the ants made a stinging march across my head to get there. I'm glad no Girl Scouts were around to hear my personal views of their beloved S'mores at that moment.

Even if I did like Girl Scouts, I wouldn't like Girl Scout cookies. At $1.50 for a small box, they really aren't that great a deal and if you're gonna pay that kind of money you might as well go to the bakery and get your cookies hot out of the oven.

Besides, I object to being nickeled and dimed by children fronting for charities and special interests. Like those kids who seem to be at every busy intersection on the weekends, sticking their jars through your car windows, asking for spare change. The Girl Scouts are even worse than that. They invade the privacy of your home, take your money and leave you with a bunch of over-priced cookies.

I was all set to ignore the two green-clad girls at my doorstep, when the insistent brats rang the bell a second time. I opened the door.

"Would you like to buy some cookies, sir?" asked one of them. She had a headful of red curls and a smile that wouldn't stop. The other one had freckles and braces and giggled as she told me about all the different choices.

Well, you know what happened next. I pulled out my wallet and gave them everything I had.

"I'll take a box of each," I said.

A Country Store Lunch

This is for everyone who likes to study their souse before they eat it.

It was lunchtime and I was hungry, driving down a back road that would offer no restaurant for miles. I was trying to figure out how long it would take me to reach the next town and its buffer zone of dueling fast-food franchises when I saw the store just ahead of me.

It doesn't matter where the store is or who owns it. Let's just say there are precious few like it around. And whenever I see one I cannot help but stop.

I sat in the car and studied the place, comfortable with the satisfaction that it possessed, at least on the outside, all the things that such a store should have. It was built of wood and had a tin roof that extended out front 15 feet or so, covering a narrow driveway and two ancient gas pumps. There was a kerosene pump on one side of the front door and a long, wooden bench on the other side, under the shade.

There was an old man in overalls sitting on the bench. He was drinking a Coca-Cola with salted peanuts floating up near the neck. He was busy studying something on the ground and every now and then he would stomp his feet. He didn't bother to look up when I got out of the car.

"Howya doin'?" I asked the man.

He looked up and grinned. He was about 70 or 80.

"Stompin' ants," he said. "Big suckers. Lots of 'em."

I paused at the door to look at the signs in the window.

"Smokey and the Bandit" was at the drive-in. There was a month-long gospel crusade featuring, this Saturday night only, the "Sunshine Brothers" and the "Happy Goodmans." Someone's dog had a 12-pup litter; half-Lab, half-Setter, "Good on cows" and free, said the sign. The Daughters of Rebecca were planning a charity bake sale with proceeds going to "our building fund."

The screen door was an advertisement for "Merita" bread and I knew before I opened it what to expect inside.

There was a three-sided counter and a single cash register, the kind where the numbers pop up like a Jack-in-the-box, not all electrified. There was a lady standing behind the counter reading a newspaper and all the way at the back of the store, behind the butcher case, was a man grinding some meat. They were the only ones in the store.

"Watcha need?" the woman asked.

"Just some lunch," I said.

"Help yourself," she said. "Grady's got some souse he just made. Show it to him, Grady."

Grady reached into the butcher case and pulled out a white pan that held a greasy, gray loaf of pork parts.

"Give me half a pound," I said and Grady sliced off a thick hunk then wrapped it up in white paper that blotched with the grease from the souse.

That's how you can tell if it's truly good souse. The stuff you get in supermarkets, when you can find it at all, is stiff and congealed and mostly preservatives and so dry that it is hard put to leave grease spots. Good souse fairly drips with grease and is usually much more interesting to look at because you can plainly distinguish which parts came from the pig's ears and which parts from the tails and toes and snouts. For some reason, they try to disguise these things in the prepackaged brands.

I grabbed some saltines and a carton of chocolate milk and would have picked up a can of Vienna sausage if it hadn't been for the generous portion of souse. Vienna (that's "Vie" as in "eye," not "Vee-enna) sausage is central to the theme of grocery store lunches.

My dad always used to buy some and take it along on fishing trips. One time he took all three of his young sons fishing in a 14-foot boat, an exercise that breeds no small amount of parental frustration. My dad had just spent about 15 minutes untangling all three of his sons' lines for at least the seventeenth time and had taken time out from cussing at us to pop open a beer and eat a can of Vienna sausage. I don't think they still do it, but back then they used to stick short inspirational messages in the sausage cans. I watched my dad as he read the message on the tiny piece of paper.

"I'll be damned. I'll just be damned," was all he could say before he started laughing so hard I thought he would cry. He handed me the piece of paper and I read it out loud to my brothers.

"Take a boy fishing today," it said.

But I passed up the Vienna sausage and headed for the check-out counter. The lady was ringing everything up when I spotted the big jar of pickled pig's feet. They were whole pig's feet, not just assorted joints and cartilege and I knew I couldn't pass them up.

"How much?" I asked.

"Sixty cents apiece," she said.

I asked for three. She fished them out, wrapped them in wax paper and stuck them in the sack with the rest of my lunch. I went outside in the driveway and sat on the bench in the shade. The old man in overalls was still there stompin' ants. I spread my lunch out on the bench. There was far more than I could eat alone.

"Want some?" I asked, pointing at the pig's feet. He said no, but when I told him I'd never eat them all he took a foot and said thanks.

"Needs some mustard," he said. "Mary, can you please throw us some mustard?"

He leaned over, opened the screen door and out flew four foil packs of mustard. He opened them all and squirted them on the wax paper.

So we sat dipping our pig's feet in mustard, watching the cars go by, stomping an ant from time to time. I figured there wasn't a better place I could have stopped for lunch.

"Good pig's foot," the old man said.

Yes, I agreed. A good pig's foot. Maybe even the best pig's foot around.

The Idea Shortage

This is a perfect example of how to write a column when you are out of ideas.

I don't want to make a big deal out of this, but I'm the person who alerted the world to the Idea Shortage.

Yeah, I know what some of you are thinking. You're thinking there's no such thing as an Idea Shortage. You're thinking it was just something dreamed up to make a few people like myself very rich and that an Idea Shortage never has existed.

All I can say is this: Go ahead and ignore the facts. Keep on using up ideas like there is no tomorrow. But sooner or later it's going to catch up with you. One morning you're going to wake up and — poof! — all the ideas will have disappeared. Don't say I didn't warn you.

Nowadays it seems almost absurd to think we once lived under the notion that the world had a limitless supply of ideas. Back in those idea-rich times we would have laughed if anyone had talked about a Creativity Crisis.

"There are more ideas in this world than we know what to do with," we would have said. "All it takes is a little creativity to find them and make them work."

Heck, that's what I thought and I was even in the idea business myself.

For years, I'd made a living by pumping a crude idea from the well each morning and refining it into an 800-word column for mass consumption by late afternoon.

I sold my ideas cheap back then. There was a glut of ideas on the world market and the going rate was barely one-tenth what it is today.

But sometime during the early 1980s, those of us in the idea business began to see the stark reality of the situation.

I guess we'd just chosen to ignore it before, but the truth became obvious. There were only so many ideas on hand from the beginning of the world and with the advent of the 20th Century's consumer-oriented society we'd been using them up at an alarming rate. Sure, it's still possible to create new ideas, but it takes a long time and, frankly, it's just not cost efficient.

I can still remember that dark morning when I sat down at the typewriter and, much to my horror, discovered I was out of ideas. I tried to draw from the stockpile, but nothing was there.

Now, I could have chosen the easy way out of my dilemma and probably gotten away with it. I could have taken an old idea and recycled it. But that goes against my nature. I don't believe in polluting the environment with stale ideas. Besides, that wasn't solving the basic problem.

So I called up my editor and gave him the news.

"Listen," I said. "There's an Idea Shortage and you won't get my column today unless a few conditions are met."

"Like what sort of conditions?" my editor asked.

"Well, starting today, you will get 10 percent fewer columns and pay 250 percent more for the ones you get," I said. "I hate to do this, but it's an economic necessity and will provide me with the resources I need to find additional idea deposits."

"You're out of your mind," my editor said. "What makes you think you can get away with this?"

"I'm just following a basic law of the marketplace," I said. "When there was a sugar shortage, the price of sugar went up. Same thing with oil, coffee and dozens of other commodities. Ideas are no exception to the rule."

"Don't give me double-talk," my editor shouted. "Either you come up with an idea and give me a column or I'll find someone else to do it."

"Go ahead and find someone else," I said.

Don't think this was a particularly bold move on my part. It wasn't. I knew I was dealing from strength.

I had already called a meeting of OWEC — the Organization of Writers and Eclectic Columnists — and we had decided to present a united front in dealing with the Idea Shortage. After all, the members of OWEC hold 90 percent of the free world's idea resources. We knew we could call the shots on how those ideas were dispensed and set a fair market price for our labors.

It was just a matter of time before the editors were calling us and begging for ideas.

Of course, we were accused of blackmail when our plans were first announced. Our fiercest critics said we were holding the people of the world as intellectual hostages, especially when the first "idea adjustments" started popping up in bills for newspapers, magazines and books.

I know this hurts your pocketbook, but, speaking for OWEC, I'd like to remind you once again that the Idea Shortage is very real and we are working desperately to get it under control. And until then, we all must share the load.

We at OWEC have your best interests in mind. We are striving to make the world idea-efficient, ridding the world of idea guzzlers who waste this precious resource.

Thanks for your cooperation and the next time you spot a good idea, enjoy it and think of OWEC.

A Brief Case For Briefcases

Show me a man with a briefcase and I will show you a man who has something to hide.

Not long ago I was asked to speak at a high school "Career Day " and "offer vocational guidance" in my "field of expertise."

I got a big kick out of this.

As I understand it, "vocational guidance" means me telling someone how to do my job. Now, I'm all for self-discovery and self-improvement and the whole batch of hyphenated, highfalutin ideals that have been trotted out and paper-trained by generation upon generation of pretentious youths. But I also believe strongly in a concept called self-preservation. In other words, I am not about to give some young kid any hints on how to do my job.

The reason for this should be obvious. Offering "vocational guidance" would be a crime. It would be aiding and abetting someone who could very well come along and steal my job. My position is precarious enough as it is without my helping the potential competition. Scratch my assistance in "vocational guidance."

As for my "field of expertise," it is not so much a field as it is, say, a tiny backyard or, better yet, a mere window box wherein a grab bag variety of seeds are scattered from time to time. Some sprout, some don't. Those few that miraculously manage to bloom do so, I assure you, by accident, not expert cultivation. Simply put: I don't have a "field of expertise."

Having eliminated "vocational guidance" and "field of expertise" as meaningful topics in my "Career Day" speech, I chose, instead, to talk about the secret to success in the working world. Since some of you who read this may be vocationally confused, I will let you in on the secret.

The secret is just one word and the word is — briefcase. That's right — briefcase.

Forget about college, advanced degrees, management training, motivational seminars and all the other garbage geared to groom for success. Simply buy a briefcase and you are on the fast track to fame and fortune.

For proof, let us examine this from a historical perspective. Who was it that invented briefcases, anyway? A lawyer, that's who.

In the days before briefcases, lawyers were no different from other working stiffs. In fact, they were held in extremely low esteem since oldtime lawyers — just like their modern counterparts — never sweated over their work and had an uncanny ability to confuse matters, rather than untangle them.

One day, a lawyer came along who decided he needed an object in which he could tote all his stuff. Now, all of us have stuff that we like to tote around with us, but lawyers apparently feel their stuff is more important than our stuff, so they have a special name for it. A lawyer's stuff is called a "brief," a peculiar piece of nomenclature since this stuff is usually anything but brief.

This enterprising, oldtime lawyer put his stuff into a handy satchel and, for lack of a better word, called it a "briefcase." And no sooner had he appeared on the streets with the world's first briefcase, than he experienced an astonishing rise in social stature. In short, he prospered. He was a success.

The reason for his success was simple. After seeing the oldtime lawyer on the street toting his briefcase, the question on everyone's mind was: "Just what in the hell does he have in there?"

No one even considered that he was toting regular, old stuff, just like everyone else's regular, old stuff. Otherwise, why would he go to all the trouble of sticking it in a special container?

"Aha," came the answer to everyone's mind, "He must be toting some very important, maybe even valuable, stuff in that handy satchel, therefore he must be treated accordingly."

In this way, a clever and profitable hoax was perpetrated upon the world, a hoax that slews of success-minded individuals have used to their great advantage ever since.

Today you will notice all kinds of people toting briefcases. And, I might add, we are all quite successful.

For instance, I walked into the office just a few minutes ago toting my briefcase. It had been some time since I had made an appearance in the office and, as you might imagine, the boss was somewhat peeved over my absence.

But before he could utter a word, I slapped my briefcase on the desk, gave the latches an impressive snap and immediately began fooling around with all the important stuff inside, important stuff like the latest copy of Sports Illustrated, my overdue tax forms, stray cigars, an 8 X 10 glossy of Cissy Spacek and a book entitled "How to Win Big at the Dog Track." All stuff, I might add, that has nothing whatsoever to do with my job. But, what the heck, I succeeded in fooling the boss and what greater success can one hope for?

All of which leads us to our moral: Remember, it's not what you tote. But how you tote it.

And on that, I rest my briefcase.

Blessed Are The Savers

I just found this old column laying around. I knew it would come in handy someday.

There are ony two kinds of people in this world— those who save things and those who don't.

I'm in the first bunch. I save everything. Care to see?

Just look inside my kitchen cabinet. See all those coffee cans? Must be eight or nine of them, with big, wide mouths and tight-fitting plastic lids. How can anyone throw out a perfectly good coffee can?

I planned to use my coffee cans for storing old grease. Yes, I save that, too. Who knows? Maybe I'll get around to making soap out of it or something. But the coffee cans leaked and the grease got all over the new dish towels and now I am saving the coffee cans for storing odds and ends.

Right now, most of the odds and ends are out in the garage. In fact, that's where all my really good stuff is.

I've got nuts and bolts and screws in every shape and size imagineable. There's some over there, scattered out across the top of the water heater. I can't remember how they got there.

Came out of an old fan or something.

Look out for those nails on the floor. They're always getting knocked off the shelves. Yeah, I know, they're rusty, but you can't ever tell when they might come in handy.

Someday I'll get around to gathering up all the nuts and bolts and screws and nails and putting them in my coffee cans. Someday when I get the time.

That's some big stack of newspapers over there, huh? I used to recycle them, but now I'm holding onto them because I understand there's this gadget you can get that will roll up your newspapers and turn them into logs for the fireplace. Waste not, want not, I always say.

Lots of stuff that's here in the garage is broken and needs to be fixed— a bicycle pump, a plant stand, a couple of sprinklers, a lamp or two, a stapler, four fishing rods, a Coleman stove and lantern, a baby stroller. Maybe I can take care of it next weekend.

Let's take a look at my bedroom closet. I have a lot of shoes. But there are only a couple of pairs that I ever wear.

The rest are back-ups. You can't ever tell when you might require an old pair of sneakers. That's why I have at least six or seven pairs.

And those black lace-ups— I wore them to my high school prom. How could anyone get rid of shoes they wore to the high school prom?

I keep a lot of things that are worth saving in my top dresser drawer. Important pieces of paper mostly. Receipts and letters and stuff like that.

Here's the receipt from when the repairman came and fixed our stove two weeks after the warranty ran out. It cost $134.79. I'm holding on to it because I intend to write an angry letter to the manufacturer, complaining about the quality of the stove.

Hmmmm. That receipt is dated last March. I really should do something about it soon.

Here's something from the insurance company explaining why my premiums were increased back in 1979. Here's a note from the babysitter that says I should call my brother. Here's a brochure that the Avon Lady left at the door last year. Here's a pamphlet about the Miami Zoo from when we visited it a while back. Here's some ads I've cut out from magazines about things I'd like to order— a kit for building your own rowboat, a corduroy sport coat from L.L. Bean, seeds for Chinese vegetables and a gadget that will roll up newspapers and turn them into logs for your fireplace.

And here's some old ticket stubs from movies I've seen in the last couple of years. I really ought to keep them awhile longer. You can't ever tell.

There are lots of other things that I'm fond of saving— paper clips, dead flashlight batteries, plastic bags, pennies, film canisters, burned out fuses, discount coupons, old postcards, theater programs, mayonnaise jars.

And I'd be glad to show you all that stuff, but I'm not quite sure where any of it is. It's bound to turn up sooner or later.

That about does it.

All that noise you hear is probably my wife. I imagine she's out in the garage going through some of my stuff and throwing it out.

Like I said, there are only two kinds of people in this world—those who save things and those who don't.

But what I want to know is this: How come we always wind up married to each other?

Name That Condo

Of course, given some of the current landscapes, there are those who would argue that Ponce de Leon got a bit carried away when he called this place "Florida" or "Abounding in Flowers."

Lately, I've been thinking about the names of places.

I grew up in a place called Leesburg. It was called Leesburg because a fellow by the name of Mr. Lee was one of the first settlers back in the 1850s.

I happened to live on Main Street, which got its name because it ran through the center of town.

One of the best names of a place I've ever been to is Show Low, Arizona. It was named after a card game. Two ranchers got to arguing about who owned a hunk of land, took a deck of cards and cut for the low card. One fellow drew the deuce of clubs and won the land. That's why the main street in Show Low, Arizona is called "Deuce of Clubs."

I like names that have some meaning behind them, names that make sense. Maybe that explains why I have such a hard time understanding how certain places in Florida get named these days.

Real estate developers are now in charge of naming the places where we live. What they do is find some land and build a bunch of houses and then dream up a cute name that will attract a lot of buyers.

I think that's the big problem with the names of places nowadays. They are just too cute.

Some of these places sound as if you should eat them instead of live in them. Cinnamon Cove. Nutmeg Bay. Blackberry Meadows.

Names that mention trees seem to be very popular. Oak Haven. Whispering Pines. Maple Estates. Aspenwood.

Never mind that most of the trees have been bulldozed to make room for the houses. Never mind that Aspens don't grow in Florida. The names sound nice.

Lone Oak Park. I've seen a couple of places with that name. We had a Lone Oak Park in Leesburg, too. It was the cemetery. You didn't pay good money to live there.

Lots of places are named after animals. Pelican Point. Quail Hollow. Deer Run. Sandpiper Ridge.

Chances are you'll never seen any of those animals around. But I guess it would be tough selling houses in Mosquito Meadows or Cockroach Manor.

Many of these modern places seem to have interchangeable names. I was looking through a newspaper the other day and saw a place called Park Grove. Then there was a Grove Park.

What is a Park Grove anyway? For that matter, what is a Grove Park? Do the people who live in these places ever think about that?

And any place that gives the hint of water seems to sell well. Emerald Isles. Seacrest. Oceanside. It's a good bet that any place that makes a big deal about water in its name, doesn't really have a lot of it and what little there is was probably imported.

Here in Florida, some of the developers get carried away naming their places with foreign phrases. Vista del Lago. Casa Grande. Villa Grande.

I've seen a place that's called Casa Villa. Casa is the Spanish word for "house." Villa is another word for "house." Would Spanish people name any of their places "House House?"

My favorite place with a Spanish name is Aqui Esta Estates. This means: "Here It is Estates." Pretty classy, huh?

And the street names in all these places are just variations on the same absurd theme. The other day I was driving through a place called Rainbow Park. Now Rainbow Park isn't such a bad name. Excessively cheerful, perhaps, but not as bad as some other places.

The developer wasn't content though. He had to give the streets such names as Happy Road, Joy Court, Serendipity Circle. Can you imagine coming home to Serendipity Circle ever night? I wouldn't be happy about it.

I'm glad they stuck to sensible names in the place where I grew up. And I'm glad that Mr. Lee wasn't named Mr. Hicks.

The Faithful Gator

For everyone who still believes in the "Year of the Gator."

These are days of hope for the Faithful Gator. Not too much hope, mind you, because although he is a Faithful Gator, he is also a Realistic Gator, a fan who is ever-mindful of history — not to mention fate and bad luck — and the way it has so naggingly held forth in the past.

Still, there is cause for great hope these last few days before the season actually begins, a time when, indeed, most anything seems possible.

"If they win the first two, then they'll be ranked in the Top Five," the Faithful Gator tells me. "Win the first four and there's no reason why they shouldn't be Number One."

Number One.

Could it be? "Sport" magazine has picked the Gators to wind up on top. Other polls give them good ranking.

But even the Faithful Gator, true and loyal though he is, knows better than to let hope grow out of sensible proportion.

"Let's just say that if they're ever going to do it, then this would seem to be the year," he tells me. "They could very well be rolling along at 5-0 and then lose to West Texas State or something. That would be just like them."

Ah, the Faithful Gator . . . the Faithful, Fatalistic Gator.

There are some things you should know about him, since he is reasonably representative of his kind.

First of all, he never actually graduated from the University of Florida, although he did go to school there for a couple of years and lived at the ATO fraternity house.

But along came World War II and he dropped out. By the time it was over he had a wife, children seemed imminent and he gave no thought to going back to school.

Still, he has returned to Gainesville each fall to watch the Gators play, to yell "Gator Bait! Gator Bait!" as the opposing team runs on the field and sway from side to side as the band plays "We Are The Boys From Old Florida." In fact, since 1946 he has missed only one game at Florida Field and that was on account of an emergency appendectomy.

From September through December his family's schedule is planned around the games of the Gators. Five years ago, his oldest son wanted to get married on Oct. 23, but that was postponed one week because it conflicted with the Auburn game. This fall, that same son and his wife have a baby boy who is due to be christened. They would like for the christening to take place in September, but the Gators play their first four games at home this season. There's no open date until October.

The Faithful Gator's pre-game ritual is as rootbound as the ivy that clings to Tigert Hall. In orange shirt and blue pants, he arrives at his parking spot several hours before game time, the same parking spot he has used for years and a meeting place for numerous other equally Faithful Gators.

His wife has been known to complain about his compulsion for such an early arrival. Still, she never fails to go all-out in her own preparation — homemade biscuits and ham, potato salad, deviled eggs and a bottomless bag of giant boiled peanuts.

At some point, the Faithful Gator takes time to fill a pint flask with bourbon, then carefully camouflages it beneath the binoculars in a small bag he straps over one shoulder. Signs at the entrances to Florida Field say "No Alcoholic Beverages Permitted," but what this really means is "Just Don't Let Us See You Bring It In."

The Faithful Gator arrives at his seats at least an hour before kickoff. He has held the same four seats for years — southwest corner, 68th row, on about the 10-yard line — and in all likelihood they will be passed down through his family. The tickets are not cheap, as much as $15 each for this year's games, not to mention the donation he must first make to the University of Florida Athletic Association for the privilege of buying the tickets. All things considered, it will cost him a couple of thousand dollars to be a Faithful Gator. But we are talking tradition here and that is beyond the thought of money.

Yet, the Faithful Gator would gladly offer every cent he could spare if he knew it would help capture that chimera-like fantasy, that ever-elusive dream known as the "Year of the Gator" — the

Southeastern Conference Championship and a shot at the national title.

He's not predicting that this is the year.

"We could go 8-3. Lose to Miami, Southern Cal and Georgia and still make it to a bowl game," he says. "But we'll beat Florida State. We'll beat the (choose your own expletive) out of Florida State. The 'Year of the Gator' though? I don't know. I just don't know."

But the season is still three days away. And for the Faithful Gator, my father, there is hope.

The Boys From Kirkland

I love Little League baseball because it provided me with my single shot at athletic glory. I once scored a home run. . . on a bunt. That's the beauty of little boys playing baseball.

I opened the Sunday paper expecting to find the story on the front page. It wasn't there.

So, I turned to the Sports section and found one small line that gave the score— Kirkland 6, Taiwan 0 — then a short story buried way back by the classified ads.

This is hardly sufficient fanfare, given the magnitude of the event that took place last Saturday in Williamsport, Pa.

That's why I'm asking all of you to join in with some applause this morning for a group of young men from Kirkland, Washington, U.S. of A., the new Little League Champions of the World.

To help you grasp the enormity of their victory, allow me to provide a bit of background.

Until the boys from Kirkland won the other day, an American team had not captured a "legitimate" Little League World Series crown since 1968.

I say "legitimate" because back in 1975, after years of foreign dominence of the American pastime, the rules were changed so that only teams from the United States could compete in the Little League World Series.

Thankfully, this dumb, poor-loser rule lasted only one year. In 1976, the series was re-opened to the rest of the world. And teams from Taiwan then won the world championship for five years in a row.

In fact, during the last 13 years of international play, the Taiwanese had lost only once, in 1970, to Nicaragua. American teams had been shut out since before the boys from Kirkland, Washington were even born.

But all that ended Saturday when Cody Webster took the mound for Kirkland.

Cody Webster is 12 years old. He stands 5-6 and weighs 174 lbs., which gives him the appearance of a blond-haired Fernando Valenzuela when he winds up and throws.

In Little League games there are only six innings, a total of 18 outs per side. Cody Webster struck out Taiwanese batters for 12 of those outs and showed some fine glove work to snare a couple more. He allowed only two hits.

As if this weren't enough, Cody Webster also hit a home run over the centerfield fence, a blast that one announcer called the longest homer he'd ever seen in a Little League World Series.

I watched the game on television from start to finish. It was the most enjoyable sporting event I've seen in a long time. It was baseball in its purest form and there's little else to compare with that.

These are not particularly good days for America's national pastime. Last year there was the player's strike with its irrepairable attack on the heart of the game. Now it seems as if the most meaningful baseball statistics are only preceded by dollar signs. And too many of the men who take part in the game, be they owners, managers or players, are more often disposed toward whining and wheeling and dealing than the basics of baseball.

But the championship game of the Little League World Series was a joy to behold.

This is not to say it was a perfect game, a game without mistakes. There were some wild throws and some passed balls and some sloppy errors.

But it was a game played with the sort of exuberance that seems to be missing from most of professional baseball. When Kirkland scored a run the dugout would unload onto the field for handshakes and back-slapping, all performed with an unabashed enthusiasm that is lacking in the big leagues. When Cody Webster slapped his homer he almost skipped around the basepaths and took a long flying leap to land smack dab on home plate.

After the final out was made — another Cody Webster strikeout — there was whooping and hollering galore. The television announcer said something about how this was "probably the greatest upset victory in sports since the American hockey team beat Russia at the winter Olympics."

I remember watching that game and, even though I'm no fan of hockey, I have to admit that I choked up a little when that final buzzer sounded.

I did the same thing Saturday after the boys from Kirkland returned the Little League World Championship to the country where it rightfully belongs.

So, hip-hip-hooray. Three cheers for Kirkland. Three cheers for the U.S. of A. And three cheers for baseball the way it's meant to be played.

I'm proud.

Mail I'll Never Get

I first started noticing a decline in the quality of my mail shortly after the phone company began urging its customers to reach out and touch someone. Do you think I could sue them for assault?

Each day when I come home there's a small pile of mail waiting for me on the dining room table.

I used to have great expectations for the mail. I used to think the small pile might actually contain something worthwhile.

But except for occasional letters from far-flung friends, my mail is boring. It's the same old thing, day after day.

So I've taken some time to think about the kind of letters I'd really like to receive. And I've decided to go ahead and write them to myself, seeing as how I'll never get them any other way.

Dear Mr. Morris: We here at the "Good Time Television Gospel Hour" have been busy praying for your soul every day. We are also busy helping the needy and doing other good works. This is just a note to let you know that we don't need any of your money to help us do our job. We're getting along just fine, thank you, and will consider it a privilege to continue praying for you free of charge. Sincerely, **Rev. Harry Welfall**

Dear Mr. Morris: Your electric bill for the month of August is $189.63. Do you think this is outrageous? If so, just mail us a check for whatever you think our service was worth. And please make sure you deduct for all the times the power went off during thunderstorms and all the food in your refrigerator thawed out. By the way, we'll be going before the Public Service Commission next month to get approval to have our rates lowered to a more reasonable level. So go ahead and use as much electricity as you want. It won't be costing you nearly as much in the future. Sincerely, **The electric company**

Dear Mr. Morris: As your representative in Congress, I thought you'd like to know what I've been doing for you lately. Truth is, I haven't done a darn thing. For the past year, I've been working my tail off to get re-elected and haven't bothered to sponsor any legislation that would help you in any way whatsoever. If, because of this, you feel you can no longer support me, then so be it. Sincerely, **Congressman Handintill**

Dear Mr. Morris: Congratulations! You may be eligible for up to $10,000 in cash and prizes ABSOLUTELY FREE and there's NO OBLIGATION! But it's only fair to say you will have to visit one of our interval ownership condominiums where you will be subjected to sleazy, hard-sell tactics by one of our money-grubbing salespeople. They will probably hound you and keep after you relentlessly so that you'll wish you never even opened this letter. So why don't you just tear it up and throw it away. Sincerely, **The Last Resort Resort**

Dear Mr. Morris: We tried to deliver a package to your house the other day, but you weren't home. We know you can't just sit around the house waiting for us to show up and we know you just hate the lines down here at our office, so why don't you give us a call and we'll deliver the package immediately. It is marked "Postage Due — $1.47." But don't worry about that. It's on the house. Sincerely, **The Post Office**

Dear Mr. Morris: In the three years that you've belonged to our book club, you've received the monthly selection each month but haven't once paid for it. We know how hard it is to remember to send in that little card saying you don't want the monthly selection and we know what a pain in the neck it is to wrap it up and send it back. So we'd like for you to just keep all thc books and don't worry about us sicking a collection agency on you. Your next selection should be arriving free of charge any day now. Happy reading! **The Book Club**

Dear Mr. Morris: It has been a real pleasure delivering your newspaper each morning for the past year. Enclosed you will find an envelope with $5 in it. Please accept this as a token of my appreciation. Sincerely,**Your newspaper carrier**

Dear Mr. Morris: Just a reminder that it's time once again for you to come in to have your teeth examined. They looked pretty good the last time and there's probably nothing wrong with them now, so if you'd like to skip this appointment then it's OK with us. Sincerely, **The dentist office**

Dear Mr. Morris: Here is your bank statement for the month of August. We noticed that a couple of times your balance slipped dangerously near the "zero" level, so we stuck in a few extra bucks to help you out. We make so much money off the interest we charge on your loans that's it's only fair we help you out when you need it. Sincerely,**The bank.**

I'm still working on the letter I'd like to receive from the IRS. I'll let you know what it says next April.

Bucking Trends With Fillmore

Whenever you worry that you aren't keeping up with the trends on the cover of Time magazine, just remember Time magazine's judgment in other issues — like naming the Ayatollah Khomeini the "Man of the Year."

A recent cover story in Time magazine showcased the growing popularity of home computers.

It is estimated that by 1985 more than 10 million American homes will rely on computers for all kinds of things.

Computers will help figure out income taxes. Computers will help balance checkbooks. Computers will help write the weekly grocery list.

But I think I can safely predict that my home won't be one of the 10 million that has a computer by 1985.

I don't make this statement out of any real objection to computers. They're OK.

It's just that around my house we're always a few giant steps behind trends that make the cover of Time magazine.

A couple of years ago, Time had a story about the growing popularity of microwave ovens. We still haven't caught up with that trend. Indeed, we're darn proud that we just stepped up to a self-cleaning oven.

I expect we'll be ready for a microwave by the turn of the century. By then, things will probably be so advanced that food will just go ahead and cook itself.

We're behind in televisions, too. The big deal these days is video cassette recorders and screens the size of picture windows.

Hey, I thought it was uptown when we made the big move to a color television not so long ago. We're now trying to decide if we're ready for remote control. I don't know. It might be too much to handle.

Given this background, it's a fair assumption that a computer does not loom on our household horizon.

Besides, I have just invested in an amazing device that, as far as I'm concerned, has it all over a computer. In fact, this device is so amazing that I can't understand why Time magazine doesn't do a cover story on it.

Let me share some of its remarkable highlights with you:

1. Unlike a computer, it is totally energy efficient. It doesn't have to be plugged into a wall socket. And it doesn't use up batteries.

2. Unlike a computer, it doesn't require an understanding of technological terms. If you know your alphabet, then you've got it licked.

3. Unlike a computer, it won't drain your bank account to buy one. If you look around, you can pick one up for less than $100.

4. Unlike a computer, it will never be rendered obsolete by generational improvements. It has reached the absolute height of its perfection.

What is this amazing device that has revolutionized my household bookkeeping and brought order to a life once fraught with chaos?

A filing cabinet. That's it plain and simple. A filing cabinet.

Not just any filing cabinet, mind you, but a four-drawer, cream-colored, steel filing cabinet with chrome handles and nifty little chrome-framed slots that display a label for each of the four drawers.

Lots of people give their computers names. I've done the same thing with my new filing cabinet. I call him Fillmore.

Fillmore has made our household truly efficient. He replaces our old, archaic way of storing information, one that is commonly known as the "P&B System." That stands for "Pile-it and Box-it." First, you pile everything up in the corners and when the piles get too high you dump them in boxes.

The "P&B Systems" works fine to a point, then you have a tough time figuring out where everything is. Your income tax forms get mixed up with old love letters and your insurance papers get crumpled in with that great novel you started but never finished and the whole thing becomes a mess.

With Fillmore everything has its place and all I have to do is stroll up, slide open a drawer and it's all at my fingertips. No muss, no fuss and, best of all, no talking back.

That's what I hate most about computers. They get sassy and talk back to you.

I speak from experience. Modern-day newspapers like the one I work for have reached the point that columnists such as myself now have to write our stories on computers.

For instance, sitting here writing this column I just punched the wrong key by mistake and the words "SYNTAX ERROR" flashed up on the screen. I pushed another button and got "EDITOR UNRECOGNIZED COMMAND." Another one and I got "PRIVILEGE VIOLATION."

Fillmore never treats me that way. The worse thing he has ever done was the other day when it was rainy and sticky out and I went to open one of his drawers and he squeaked a little. I shot him up with WD-40 and everything was fine.

Quite a device, ol' Fillmore. I don't think he'll ever be replaced.

Why I Live Here

*I once thought about moving out of Florida. . .
for about two seconds.*

Not long ago, an out-of-state visitor asked me why I live down here in this corner of Florida. It was a good question, one I've often asked myself, so I tried to answer it.

I mumbled something about the climate and the Gulf of Mexico and the beaches and the sunsets.

I mentioned the good fishing and good sailing and good bars and good restaurants and good friends to share it all with.

I said I like it here because it is safe distance from Miami, Orlando, Tampa and other places where, generally speaking, I do not get along well.

I think I satisfied the out-of-town visitor. But the more I got to thinking about it, I didn't really tell him the true reason why I live here.

If you get right down to it, the true reason is latitude. I repeat: Latitude.

I know this demands some explanation. Allow me to provide it in the form of a mathematical equation:

$27^\circ L = L_1 = I$

Don't worry. This isn't nearly as complicated as it seems. It's quite simple, actually, if you plug in the following definitions.

Let **L** stand for latitude in a geographic sense, meaning the parallel lines that go east-west around the globe, intersecting the longitude lines.

Let **27°** represent the approximate location, latitude-wise, where, if you were driving north to south, you would first begin to experience the benefits down here. In other words, any latitudinal location below 27° would fit into the equation. For the record, the latitude of Fort Myers is 26.37° North. Sarasota is roughly 27° North.

Let L_1 stand for latitude in a social sense, meaning, according to Webster's, "freedom of action or choice."

And finally, let **I** stand for inertia, meaning, once again according to Webster's, "the indisposition to motion, exertion or change."

Now, given these definitions, we can easily use them to construct an intelligible sentence in Mother English. A most literal translation of the equation $27^\circ L = L_1 = I$ would be: "If one is lucky enough to live anywhere below 27°L, then one will experience great freedom of action that invariably results in an indisposition to move or exert one's self."

In other words, there ain't no problem about taking life easy down here. Truth is, you HAVE to take it easy; to do otherwise would mean violating a universal law of nature.

Simply put, this law of nature states that as one gets closer to the equator the slower one's metabolism becomes. I don't know how or why this works, but it does. A whole slew of natural forces are probably responsible for it — gravity, tides, the sun, the moon.

For proof, just look at how people act up north. They're jumpy. They fidget and squirm and bustle around, often bustling simply for the sake of bustling. They cannot help this perpetual state of momentum. They are sad victims of their own latitude.

Heading south, the pace slackens. State by state, latitude line by latitude line, subtle changes take place until, in that region known as the Deep South, slowness truly sets in.

The quality of this slowness is pretty much uniform throughout the Deep South until one approaches the magic 27 latitude marker, where everything begins to change, where a bit of exotica is added to the slowness.

This exotica results from the fact that, living here in southernmost Florida, we are not a part of the Deep South. We are not really even a part of the rest of Florida. Instead, our identification lies with the Carribean, with the islands, with the tropics.

And here in the tropics, in the lower latitudes, we are bound by our very location to relax. Once relaxed, we can enjoy the full range of social latitudes, imbibe in those freedoms that come with the terrain.

And once we learn to take advantage of the latitude, it is a simple matter to slip easily into a state of inertia. Inertia is not a bad thing. It is not to be confused with laziness or lethargy. Rather, inertia is the ability to set one's self up in the best of all possible situations and then stay there while exerting the least bit of effort imagineable. It's the most pleasing level of existence available to mankind.

Unfortunately, many people who move down here to the tropics are not prepared for the full scope of changes they must undergo to reach inertia. They remain tied to the rhythms and motions of more temperate climes, to the fast-paced life. They insist on running in high gear, while they really needn't shift out of low.

I live here because my transmission is stuck in low gear and, thankfully, in this corner of Florida, there's no chance of getting it repaired. Besides, I'm at a point of equilibrium. If I moved any further north, I'd have to shift gears or get run down. Any further south and I'd probably come to a complete stop and rust.

As it is, I just putter contentedly along, wasting no gas, getting nowhere fast and having one helluva good time.

It's just a simple matter of latitude and inertia.

$\mathbf{27^\circ L = L_I = I}$

That says it all.

Bob Morris is a fourth generation Floridian, born and raised in Leesburg. A graduate of the University of Florida, he joined the Fort Myers News-Press in October 1975. His work has won a number of national awards, including honors from the National Press Club and the National Headliner's Club. He is also a recipient of the Scripps-Howard Foundation's Ernie Pyle Award for outstanding human interest writing in America. He and his wife, Debbie, live in Lee County with their two sons, Bo and Dash.

More, more, more . . .

Like what you've just read? Want to share it with a friend?

Then we here at Soggy Cracker Press have some kind of deal for you. Now you can send a copy of "Greetings from Florida" or Bob Morris's first book, "True Floridians & other passing attractions" and enjoy a special discount on your orders.

Buy one copy of either book for $6.95 and each additional book you'd like is only $5. This includes all postage, tax and handling. If you order two books, then you save almost $2.

In case you aren't familiar with "True Floridians & other passing attractions," let's just say that it's a collection of 56 short essays upon such topics as what it takes to become a True Floridian, how to properly deal with mosquitoes and the true story of why Adam and Eve were kicked out of the Garden of Eden because of mango lust.

Just fill out the handy-dandy coupon below and mail it to:

SOGGY CRACKER PRESS
P.O. BOX 10
FORT MYERS, FL 33902

Yes, for some strange reason, I want to share Bob Morris's books with my friends. I hope they'll forgive me. Enclosed is my check or money order for $6.95, plus $5 for each additional book that I choose.

I want____ copy(ies) of "Greetings from Florida."
I want____ copy(ies) of "True Floridians & other passing attractions."

I've enclosed a separate sheet of paper with the names and addresses of my friends or you can send everything to me:

Name ______________________________

Street Address ________________________

City ____________ **State** ______ **Zip** ______

(Guaranteed delivery in a plain, brown wrapper.)